THE U.S. MARINES
IN ACTION

VILLARD
MILITARY SERIES

THE U.S. MARINES
IN ACTION

Series Editor: Ashley Brown

Consultant Editors:

Brigadier-General
James L Collins Jr (Retd)

Dr John Pimlott

Brigadier-General
Edwin H Simmons USMC (Retd)

VILLARD BOOKS NEW YORK
1986

11/88
5.00

Contributing Authors

Ashley Brown
William Dabney
Dr V. Keith Fleming
Paul Szuscikiewicz

Acknowledgments

Photographs were supplied by:
Associated Press, Camera Press, Communist Party Picture Library, Carina Dvorak, Robert Hunt Library, John Hillelson Agency, Imperial War Museum, Orbis Publishing, Tim Page, The Photo Source, Photri, Popperfoto, The Research House, Rex Features, Edwin H Simmons, Frank Spooner Pictures, UPI/Bettmann, US Air Force, US Army, US Marine Corps, US Navy.

Back cover photograph: US Marines on parade, Beirut 1983
Title spread: US Marine, Grenada 1983

Library of Congress Catalog Card Number: 85-40981
ISBN: 0-394-74402-0

Printed in Italy
9 8 7 6 5 4 3 2
First Edition

CONTENTS

INTRODUCTION
The US Marine Corps 1798-1945

ON 6 JUNE 1918, World War I was in its decisive phase. The German Army had launched a series of spring offensives intended to force Britain and France to the negotiating table before the arrival of large numbers of American troops tipped the balance against Germany. The defeat of Russia had released many battle-hardened veterans from the Eastern Front, and these had spearheaded the German attacks. Their successes against war-weary British and French troops had brought them to within 40 miles of Paris.

The pressure of the German advances demanded that all available Allied troops be rushed to the front lines. US forces, whose use had been restrained by the American demand to fight as a single, national army, were now released to go into action where they were needed most. One unit, the Marine Brigade of the 2nd Infantry Division, left its camp in Normandy and journeyed to the Marne river sector. The German forces in the area occupied strong defensive positions in the wooded terrain. One particularly tough bastion was the Bois de Belleau (Belleau Wood).

Below: US troops move forward through barbed-wire. The bags slung over their shoulders contain grenades, a useful weapon in the trench fighting of World War I.

The Marines were ordered to attack Belleau Wood and clear the Germans out, as part of general Allied offensive operations to drive the Germans away from Paris. An earlier attack on 6 June had seized Hill 142, which overlooked the wood from the west. The main attack went in at 1700 hours. There were three prongs: 3rd Battalion, 5th Marines attacked from the west; 3rd Battalion, 6th Marines struck at the southern end of the wood; while 2nd Battalion, 6th Marines hit the village of Bouresches.

The Marines advanced in the thick skirmish lines more typical of 1914 than 1918. The Germans opened fire with their machine guns, aiming for the legs, while shells began to explode above and around the advancing Americans. Among the soldiers of the 3rd Battalion, 5th Marines crossing a wheatfield towards the wood was Sergeant Merwin Silverthorn, later to become a Marine general. As he recounted events later, he and his platoon then advanced down a ravine. Near the bottom he came under heavy machine-gun fire and ducked behind a pile of wood. The platoon commander ordered a charge across the ravine and Silverthorn and the rest of the men rushed over. When they reached the other side, the 52 men had been reduced to six. The platoon commander, an army lieutenant, retreated, but Sergeant

The badge of the US Marine Corps, known as the 'globe and anchor', is shown above. The globe displays the western hemisphere, complementing the Royal Marines' badge, which shows the eastern hemisphere. The Marine Corps has developed a number of traditions in its long history. The Corps Hymn refers to 'the shores of Tripoli' and 'the Halls of Montezuma'; the former refers to the Eaton expedition to North Africa in 1805, and the latter commemorates the storming of the Hill of Chapultepec, an important battle of the Mexican-American War of 1846–47. The dress sword worn by officers is based on the design of a Mameluke sword presented by the Pasha of Tripoli to Lieutenant Presley O'Bannon, commander of the Marines on the Eaton expedition. Another revered institution is the Marine Corps Band, which has performed on ceremonial occasions since 1800. Under the direction of John Philip Sousa from 1880 to 1892, it toured the country, popularising many of Sousa's marches including the official Marine Corps march, *Semper fidelis*.

Silverthorn went on. He joined up with the remnants of another platoon and began moving across another wheatfield in the direction of the wood, this time in short rushes. Silverthorn was hit in the knee and lay in the field for a while, eventually making his way back to a dressing station to the rear. Few men of the 5th Marines reached the woods, most falling victim to the German machine guns.

The 3rd Battalion, 6th Marines was better placed for an attack and two companies managed to reach the woods and establish a bridgehead. A small group of Marines manned two captured machine guns and kept a Marine outpost in Belleau Wood despite German counterattacks.

The main target for the 2nd Battalion, 6th Marines was

Below: A machine-gun platoon advances cautiously through a wood in World War I.

Bouresches, the village at the southeast corner of the woods. Another wheatfield had to be crossed to reach the objective, and once again the advancing Marines came under heavy machine-gun fire. Second Lieutenant Clifton Cates, commander of the 4th Platoon, 96th Company (and later to become Marine Corps Commandant), was hit in the helmet by a Maxim round while crossing the wheatfield. Stunned, he lay on the ground until he recovered his senses. Donning his now dented helmet he made his way to four Marines he had spotted in the ravine. They started to treat his headwound by applying wine to it, but, in a phrase cherished in Marine lore, Cates exclaimed: 'Goddam it, don't pour that wine over my head, give me a drink of it.' He then picked up a French rifle and led the men into Bouresches. He reached the village in company with First Lieutenant James Robertson and 30 men. In street-fighting seven became casualties. The remainder held the village for half an hour until reinforcements arrived.

At nightfall, the survivors of the three-battalion attack dug

Below: A Marine on service in China, wearing winter dress, in the early years of this century. The Corps served in China throughout the 19th century, defending the property of US merchants.

in. The Marines held a small part of the wood, and much of Bouresches. Casualties had been heavy, nearly 1100 men, over a tenth the number that crossed the startline. The attack was not tactically brilliant, for the Marines had ignored the lessons learnt by the European powers after years of trench warfare; it was, however, a victory won by sheer courage and determination, and it gave a much-needed boost to Allied morale. It was also an historically significant event, for it demonstrated what the role of the US Marine Corps was to be in the wars of the 20th century, namely that of a tough assault force for difficult missions.

The US Marine Corps had its origins in the many units of Marines that came into being during the War of Independence (1775–83). These were small groups of fighting men formed at various times to serve aboard specific ships. From vantage points high up in the masts they would fire sniping shots at the decks of enemy vessels. Marines also participated in landings on British-held coasts, although these

Below: Marines escort a quartermaster's truck from the docks at Vera Cruz in 1914. A detachment was sent to the Mexican city to protect US oil interests during a civil war.
Below, far right: In 1931 US Marines were sent to Managua, Nicaragua, to prevent looting after an earthquake had laid waste the city.

could hardly be compared with the amphibious landings of the future.

The Marine Corps was officially established by Act of Congress on 11 July 1798, when President John Adams signed the bill into law. They were still conceived as a force to provide a fighting military element aboard ships. They were soon in action against French vessels in an undeclared naval war fought in the West Indies from 1798 to 1801. This conflict was followed by the war declared against the Pasha of Tripoli by President Thomas Jefferson in 1803. Marines fought in several actions, including the famous Eaton expedition of 1805. Starting from the Nile, 100 men (eight of whom were Marines) marched 600 miles across the Libyan desert to besiege and storm the Tripolitan town of Derna. Eaton and his men took the town and held it for six weeks until the war

came to an end. A treaty was signed which terminated the tribute previously paid to the Pasha.

During the war of 1812 Marines once again served primarily in small units on board ships. However, a combined unit of sailors and Marines made a name for themselves in the battle of Bladensburg in 1814. This action is notorious for the rapid flight of the main body of American forces, leaving the Marines and sailors to act as a fighting rearguard against the British forces marching on Washington.

As with the US Navy, to join the Marines was also to see the world. Marines travelled to the Far East, to Africa, to Europe and the Mediterranean, protecting the interests of American commerce and showing the flag. They also played a leading role in the Mexican-American War of 1846–47, serving as a battalion of the force led by General Winfield Scott against Mexico City. They became famous for their storming of Chapultepec, a military school, which involved savage hand-to-hand fighting.

However, like the rest of the American military establishment, the Marines were disrupted by the outbreak of the Civil War in 1861, and many officers quit the Corps to fight for the Confederate Army. During the war, the Marines never found a satisfactory role for themselves. The Confederate Navy was minuscule and there were few ship-to-ship battles in which the Marines' traditional skills could come to the fore. In a few incidents, Marines formed *ad hoc* battalions for fighting in the line of battle, but they were undistinguished in action. Thus, when Congress was considering budget cuts in

One of the most famous World War II Marine Aviation units was VMF-214, known as 'The Black Sheep', whose badge is shown above. The first US Marine to undergo flight training qualified as a pilot in 1912, but when the US entered World War I in 1917, there were no more than 39 Marine aviators. However, the unit was expanded quickly, and four squadrons were serving with British and French units by the end of the war. Between the wars Marine aviation units participated in the many interventions in the Caribbean, and new techniques of dive-bombing and ground support were tried in combat. Marine aviation was reorganised when the Corps was expanded in February 1941 and redesignated the 1st and 2nd Marine Aircraft Wings. By January 1945 there were five Air Wings with 10,412 pilots and a total of 132 squadrons. The Marines were supplied with helicopters in 1948 and in 1952 the number of Air Wings was permanently fixed by law at three.

1866 (because of the cost of the recent war), disbanding the Corps was seriously considered.

The Marines survived, however, and throughout the rest of the 19th century played an important role in the rise of the United States to the status of a world power. They protected American business interests both at home (suppressing labour riots in 1877) and abroad (with landings in Egypt, Korea, and Latin America). In 1898 these activities culminated in the war with Spain, through which the United States acquired the colonies of Puerto Rico, the Virgin Islands and the Philippines. The Philippines provided a new theatre of action for the Corps, as nationalist rebels resisted the imposition of US control. Marines were also part of the

Above: Marines wade ashore at Tarawa during the battles for the Gilbert Islands in 1943. The war in the Central Pacific was dominated by the amphibious landings made by the Corps. The bloody fighting in the Gilberts taught the Marines many lessons that were applied during the battles for the Marianas in 1944. The purpose of these thrusts across the Pacific was to acquire air bases for the bombing of Japan, as well as isolating the Japanese forces in the Philippines and the Dutch East Indies.
Right: The famous second flag-raising ceremony on Mount Suribachi on Iwo Jima. It is commemorated by the Marine Corps monument in Washington, D.C.

western forces that dealt with the attacks on foreign legations during the Boxer Rebellion of 1900 in China. It was in this hectic period that they first acquired the nickname 'Leathernecks' – a reference to the leather collar-stiffeners that were a distinctive feature of the 19th-century uniform.

The Marines were still not accepted as a fixed part of the US military establishment, however; before World War I, there were again attempts to disband the Corps, and even President Teddy Roosevelt supported such moves. Nevertheless, the success of the Marine units involved in World War I, and especially the victory at Belleau Wood, put the Marines firmly on the map, and there were few calls for their disbandment after 1918.

Haiti, Cuba, and Nicaragua – all felt the weighty presence of the Leathernecks

In the 1920s and 1930s too, the Marines were kept busy, for intervention in the affairs of Central American and Caribbean nations was constant. Haiti, Cuba and especially Nicaragua (where Marines fought guerrillas led by Augusto Sandino from the late 1920s until 1933) – all felt the weighty presence of the Leathernecks. There was a return to China, too, as the confused situation there led to a detachment being dispatched to Shanghai in the late 1920s.

By the mid-1930s, the threat of world war was again looming on the horizon. Not only was Nazi Germany casting shadows; Japanese ambitions in China and the Pacific were clearly a threat to US interests. The Marines began experimenting and preparing for the type of fighting that they believed they would encounter in any future Pacific War – a war that was soon forced on them.

Marines were involved in World War II from 1941 to 1945,

The battle of Iwo Jima is celebrated by the Marine Corps as one of its toughest actions. Its strategic value was as an emergency landing strip for the B-29s bombing Japan from the Marianas. Three Marine divisions were committed against the 23,000 Japanese troops who had honeycombed the island with bunkers and tunnels to strengthen their position. The Marines landed on 19 February 1945 at the narrowest point on the island, intending to cut the Japanese positions in two. In four days of heavy fighting the Marines captured the southern part of the island, and the 5th Marine Division (whose badge is shown above) took Mount Suribachi, its highest peak. Fighting for the northern part of Iwo Jima continued until 26 March. Twenty-two Marines won Medals of Honor on Iwo, over one-quarter of the total won by the Corps in World War II. A total of 23,303 casualties made it the costliest battle in Marine history.

Above: Keeping a tight grip on his M1 carbine, a Marine of the 5th Marine Division radios for reinforcements during the savage fighting for Iwo Jima. Commenting on the sheer grit and determination shown by the Marines on the island, Admiral Chester W. Nimitz paid them the ultimate tribute: 'Among the Americans who served on Iwo Jima, uncommon valor was a common virtue.'

taking part in many of the most important campaigns in the Pacific and developing techniques that pushed amphibious warfare to new levels. The first notable Marine action was on Wake Island, where a small garrison (only 449 Marines) held off Japanese assaults for 16 days in December 1941 before eventually succumbing to overwhelming numbers. Marines were involved too in the defence of the Bataan peninsula in the Philippines, and were part of the garrison of Corregidor when it fell in May 1942.

After these early US defeats, the Marines moved onto the offensive, although they often found the going hard. In August 1942, Major-General Alexander Vandegrift's 1st Marine Division went ashore on Guadalcanal, starting a long campaign that wrested the initiative away from the Japanese in the Solomons. The dour struggle on Guadalcanal established and confirmed the Marine tradition.

In 1943, Marines participated in the drive up the Solomons chain, but perhaps the most important battle of that year was thousands of miles away in the Gilberts, where Marine units suffered heavy losses in taking the small atoll of Tarawa. The experience of Tarawa showed senior Marine officers that they needed to tighten up their procedures in dealing with a tenacious foe like the Japanese, and that the equipment they used to land troops had to be vastly improved. The lessons learnt at Tarawa were to bring about a new approach that worked wonders in the years ahead.

The Marine forces worked mainly with the Central Pacific axis of US advance, under Admiral Nimitz, rather than with the South Pacific forces of General MacArthur, and in 1944 they moved against the two island chains that opened a way directly towards the Japanese home islands: in February the Marshalls were attacked, and then, in the summer, the Marianas, the latter offering unrivalled bases for air attacks on Japan. The fighting for the Marianas was hard, particularly for the island of Saipan, but once more the Marines triumphed.

After a bloody but victorious assault on the island of Peleliu in the Palau group in September 1944, the next major action for the Marines was on the island of Iwo Jima in February 1945. This small volcanic outcrop was the scene of one of the most famous single incidents of the war, when Marines raised the American flag over the summit of Mount Suribachi, an extinct volcano that had dominated the landing beaches and cost hundreds of lives to take.

The final large-scale battle for the Marines was on Okinawa in April 1945, where last-ditch Japanese defenders had once more to be winkled out, one by one. This was one of the most dangerous tasks of the war, for every rock could conceal a fanatical foe, determined to give his life in the service of his emperor. Marines prepared for the invasion of Japan itself after the fall of Okinawa – most were probably relieved when the atomic bombs brought the war to a close.

By the end of World War II, there were almost 485,000 Marines in the Corps. 19,733 Marines had died, and 67,207 had been wounded in action – almost all in the Pacific War.

1

A SEESAW STRUGGLE
The Marines in Korea

THE KOREAN WAR

The Korean War had two phases: a year of movement and two years of stalemate. It began in June 1950 with a North Korean offensive that reached the far south of the peninsula; this was countered by United Nations forces (mainly US troops) pushing far into North Korea; and, late in 1950, these were driven back, in their turn, by Chinese intervention. It was in this period that the Marines conducted their retreat from the Chosin reservoir. When the Chinese offensive ran out of steam, a UN offensive (codenamed 'Killer' and then 'Ripper') forced the communists north. A further communist offensive in late spring 1951 was soon blocked, and the US troops moved north again, to establish a line roughly along the original border. There followed two years of stalemate, in which even large-scale battles failed to break the deadlock. The Marines lost 4262 dead and 21,781 wounded in Korea, and the 1st Marine Division remained in South Korea until 1955. A total of 258 Marine aviators were killed and 174 wounded, and 436 Marine aircraft were lost.

LATE IN the afternoon of 27 November 1950, in pitch darkness, units of the 5th Marine Regiment were huddled in their tents and foxholes near Yudam-ni, in northeast Korea, one of the most inhospitable places they could possibly have chosen. They were expecting trouble – and they certainly got it. Enemy patrols suddenly appeared, and a rain of mortar shells on the forward positions signalled an all-out assault. Staff Sergeant Robert Kennemore, who had fought on Guadalcanal, desperately tried to rally his platoon. He was directing a machine-gun team when a grenade suddenly landed in the position. Kennemore put his foot on it to minimise the effect of the explosion – and lost both his legs. He was later awarded the Medal of Honor; and Kennemore's hard-pressed men held out.

The 1st Marine Division displayed dogged, unflinching courage

This selfless and heroic action typified the Marines' spirit during one of the most astonishing achievements of the Korean War: the campaign that climaxed in the retreat from Chosin reservoir. Trained to act as an assault force, the 1st Marine Division displayed dogged, unflinching courage as it pulled back under enormous enemy pressure, and survived to play a vital part in the rest of the conflict.

In the aftermath of World War II, the Marine Corps had naturally been cut back severely; from a strength of 485,000 at the end of hostilities its personnel had dropped to under 100,000 by 1947. The Marines also had to fight off pressure that they should be absorbed into the US Army or Navy establishments. Such demands had powerful supporters, who argued that in an atomic age, there was little need for a specialised amphibious force; but the Marines managed to resist this pressure. The National Defense Act of 1947 enshrined the Marine Corps as a separate service within the Department of Defense.

The Pusan perimeter

Kumchon

Pohang-dong

Yongchon

Kuryongpo-ri

Taegu
EUSAK
HQ

Kyongju

Naktong River

Ulsan

Naktong
Bulge

Yongsan

Samnangjin

Naktong River

Nan River

Masan

Pusan

United Nations Command
front line positions
mid Sept 1950

In June 1950, therefore, when the forces of the North Korean People's Army (NKPA) attacked the much less well equipped units of the Republic of Korea (RoK) – the political authority in the southern part of the peninsula – there were Marines available to go to the aid of the South. As the USA, formally backed by the United Nations, sent in its forces to try to stem the tide of communist advance, the 1st Provisional Marine Brigade, under Brigadier-General Edward A. Craig, moved into the far south of Korea, into the so-called 'Pusan Perimeter'. Here General Walton Walker was desperately trying to retain some kind of presence within the peninsula, under severe pressure from rampant NKPA forces that had flooded down across the 38th Parallel, the prewar frontier.

The 1st Provisional Marine Brigade was under-strength (with only two rifle companies per infantry battalion rather

Page 15: Marines use scaling ladders placed against the ramp of their landing craft to get over the sea wall at Inchon.
Above: A Marine recoilless rifle crew fires at a North Korean strongpoint.
Below: US M4A3E8s (known as 'Easy Eights') give fire support to Marines near Inchon.

Above: Colonel Lewis 'Chesty' Puller commanded the 1st Marine Regiment at Inchon and during the retreat from the Chosin reservoir.

than the standard three), but it included in its complement weapons that were to make a big difference to the struggle: M-26 Pershing tanks that were able to take on the Russian-built T-34s that the North Korean forces were using to devastating effect. The Marines were deployed as part of Task Force Kean, and led a counterattack that Walker hoped would reduce the pressure that was building up. Pushing forward in unfamiliar conditions, the Marines took heavy casualties but in four days managed to push the enemy back 22 miles.

Having shown that they could handle themselves in battle, even though many of them had never before been under fire, the Marines were deployed to a critical sector. Walker sent them to the Naktong river front, where the area known as the 'Bulge' was threatened by NKPA attacks. A British military observer described these new heirs to the Marine tradition: '. . . these Marines have the swagger, confidence and hardness that must have been in Stonewall Jackson's Army of the Shenandoah.'

The fighting for the Naktong Bulge was hard. The North Koreans knew that they had a chance of final victory – the Marines knew they had to hang on. Positions changed hands many times, but the Marines won through. They pushed back the NKPA 4th Division and reoccupied the Bulge at a cost of 344 casualties. Although withdrawn in preparation for a move to Japan to join the 1st Marine Division that was forming up to carry out an amphibious landing further up the

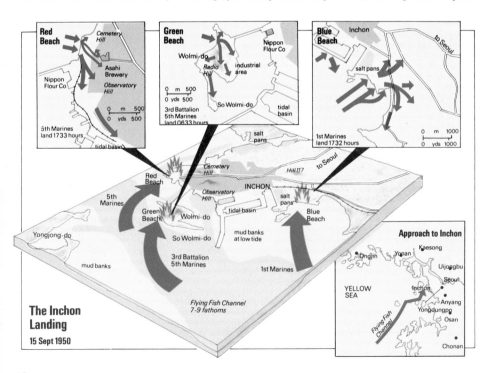

The Inchon Landing
15 Sept 1950

peninsula, the Marines in the Pusan Perimeter were soon in action again. Before they could embark for Japan, further NKPA units entered the Naktong Bulge, and the Leathernecks were thrown back into the fight. In weather that was often too bad to permit air support, tank fought it out with tank, and the offensive was slowed. The 1st Provisional Marine Brigade was now finally pulled out of the line in Pusan, and sent back to prepare for more offensive action. Along with Marine Air Group 33 (which had flown 995 close-support missions) it had played a central part in the defence of the perimeter.

The Marines had to go ashore and hold the island until the next tide

The Marines from Pusan were to join the 1st Marine Regiment from Japan as part of Major-General Oliver P. Smith's 1st Marine Division, detailed to undertake the amphibious landings at Inchon, on the west coast of the peninsula, near the South Korean capital of Seoul. This was to be the master-stroke of General Douglas MacArthur, who was pushing the scheme through in the face of opposition from all sides.

There were many difficulties involved in landing troops at Inchon – notably the problem that the tide was only high enough for three hours, and so the assault to secure a beach-head had to take place in two stages. The crucial time

Below: Four LSTs unload supplies at Inchon on 15 September 1950. The Marines secured the beachhead quite easily, and established a secure base on the first day of the landings. The gap between high and low tide was so great that the Marines had only one day to secure a foothold, or be left in an extremely precarious position until the next period of high water in October.

In Korea in 1950 the commander of X Corps, of which the 1st Marine Division was a major part, was Major-General Edward Almond (above, right), formerly a member of MacArthur's staff in Tokyo. Commanding the 1st Marine Division was Major-General Oliver P. Smith (above, left) – who had little confidence in his superior. After the Inchon landings, Almond tried to push Smith's men in a rush to Seoul, trying to 'do a Patton' (as the Marines saw it), without realising the problems involved. Later, when the Marines were deployed in northeast Korea, Smith wrote to the Marine Commandant (chief of the entire USMC) expressing serious misgivings: 'I have little confidence in the tactical judgment of the corps [X Corps] or in the realism of their planning. . . .' When the Chinese attacked in force, Almond, then in Tokyo, ordered an immediate withdrawal, abandoning heavy equipment if need be. Smith replied stiffly that he would not abandon any equipment he could use, and would withdraw only as rapidly as he could carry his wounded. The final problem arose when the Marines reached Hungnam. Smith believed he could hold a perimeter during the winter; Almond ordered the Marines to be evacuated. For the Marines, deployment in X Corps had not been a rewarding experience.

would be the first few hours: the 3rd Battalion of the 5th Marine Regiment would have to go ashore to take a feature called Wolmi-do island. They would then have to hold the island until the next tide, later that day, enabled the main landings to take place.

In the event, the landings at Inchon were a great success, and NKPA units were taken completely by surprise. The 5th Marines on Wolmi-do were never in serious trouble; and further units of the 5th Marines on Red Beach reached their objectives easily. On Blue Beach, the other main landing area, there were difficulties for the 1st Marine Regiment, which was an untried unit (unlike the 5th Marines which, as part of the 1st Provisional Marine Brigade, had been blooded at Pusan), but the problem lay in logistics rather than enemy resistance. By the evening of the following day, the whole town of Inchon was secure.

Marines now spearheaded the drive out of Inchon, to the airport at Kimpo and towards the city of Seoul. On 18 September, Kimpo was in US hands – but Seoul, an important propaganda target, was still held by NKPA forces. The Marines of Smith's 1st Division, part of X Corps under Major-General Almond, were ordered to take Seoul by 25 September; but it was not until that date that the Marines were actually fighting within the city. Desperate to hold Seoul, NKPA units began to launch heavy counterattacks – but these only showed the expertise of the Marines in coordinating their tactics.

In one incident, for example, early in the morning of 26 September, a strong NKPA force of tanks and self-propelled guns struck from the city centre against the 1st Marine Regiment. A patrol under Corporal Charles E. Collins made contact with the enemy force, and while Collins covered them, his men swiftly pulled back to inform the frontline defences, under Major Edwin H. Simmons. Although his radio operator was killed beside him in the first attack, Simmons stayed at his post, coordinating artillery fire on the enemy column. Within a short space of time, seven NKPA tanks had been destroyed and almost 500 enemy troops killed. The counterattack had been stopped in its tracks, by soldiers who knew what they were doing and who were able to work unflinchingly under fire.

The Marines were fighting off the last desperate lunges of a defeated enemy

By 29 September, the Marines were fighting off the last desperate lunges of a defeated enemy, and, with the breakout of the UN forces trapped in the Pusan Perimeter, the NKPA was in precipitate retreat throughout Korea. In true Marine tradition, the 1st Marine Division had acted as the spearhead of an assault that had reversed an unpromising strategic situation. With casualties of 2500 (plus 11 Marine Air Wing aircraft shot down), Smith's division had led the UN forces to a conclusive victory.

The RoK government of Syngman Rhee was determined to use the victory that had just been won to crush the northern

Far left: A US soldier takes aim at an enemy sniper during the battle for Seoul. Colonel Puller's 1st Marines were involved in heavy fighting around Seoul railroad station and along Ma-Po Boulevard.

Below: Amphibious craft land Marines at Wonsan. The North Koreans had laid extensive minefields off the harbour and beaches. While waiting for them to be cleared, the transports carrying the Marines were forced to sail back and forth offshore, which caused the Marines to name the landing Operation Yo-Yo.

Above: Colonel Homer Litzenberg, commander of the 7th Marines. His regiment was heavily engaged in the opening battles around the Chosin reservoir.

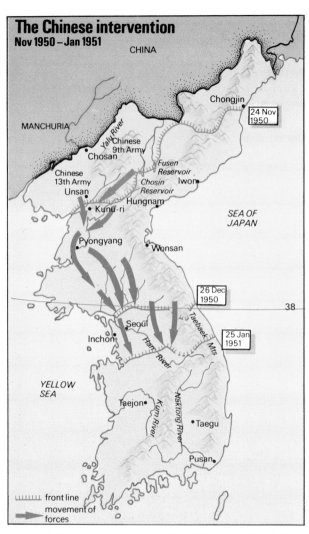

communist government for good, and General MacArthur was likewise in favour of pursuing the NKPA forces back across the 38th Parallel. The US government agreed to this strategy, and so plans were made for a large-scale offensive into the North. The 1st Marine Division, still part of X Corps under Major-General Almond, was to operate on the east side of Korea's spine-like range of mountains, while the bulk of US forces were to advance up the west side.

The Marines' first task was to have been an amphibious landing behind enemy lines at Wonsan. But as the NKPA pulled back rapidly, RoK Army troops were able to march unopposed into the town on 10 October, before the Marine landing craft had even set out. Wonsan harbour had been thoroughly mined, and not until the 25th could the Marines get ashore – in a thoroughly anti-climactic operation. Smith's division now consisted essentially of the 1st, 5th and 7th Marine Regiments, organised into regimental combat teams that could operate independently. The 1st Regiment began securing the perimeter around Wonsan, but NKPA units began a campaign of harassment and small-scale raids from the hills. Operations in the mountains were difficult; the 1st Regiment, for example, had to maintain communications from Wonsan to an important road junction at Majon-ni along a route that passed through a 3000ft-deep mountain pass, where the gorges and hairpin bends made security a nightmare – it was soon christened 'Ambush Alley'.

From Wonsan, Smith was ordered to move two of his regiments still further north, to land at Hungnam and advance towards the Yalu river via the Chosin reservoir. The first to move was the 7th Marine Regiment, under Colonel Homer L. Litzenberg ('Litz the Blitz' to his men), and as this unit fought its way towards the town of Koto-ri south of the reservoir, Smith moved Lieutenant-Colonel Raymond Murray's 5th Regiment into the fray. By 16 November, both these regiments had reached Hagaru, and Smith was allowed to bring up the 1st Regiment, under Colonel Lewis B. ('Chesty') Puller, to safeguard their communications back to Hungnam.

Already the Marines had come across Chinese forces barring their way forward; but it was thought that these were isolated examples, and that China would not dare put in sufficient units to halt the US advance. Indeed, as late as 26 November, Major-General Almond ordered Smith's

Below: Chinese troops charge past abandoned US trucks and artillery pieces. The Chinese attacks in November 1950 caught the United Nations' forces in Korea by surprise and isolated the Marine forces around the Chosin reservoir.

Right: A Marine Corsair drops napalm on a Chinese position during the retreat from the Chosin reservoir.

Below: Marines move in convoy through sub-zero temperatures during their retreat from Koto-ri to the coast.

Marines to push west from the Chosin reservoir towards the Yalu river – some 100 miles distant.

On the night of 25 November, units of the Eighth Army on the west side of the peninsula had suffered heavily under Chinese attack, and on the night of the 27th it was the turn of the 1st Marine Division. The equivalent of four army corps massed against the US forces. The attacks came not only on the forward troops: the Chinese were determined to cut off the US Marines by slicing through their fragile communications with the coast, and especially along the stretch of road between Koto-ri and Hagaru. A mixed force of Marines, British Royal Marines, and US Army troops, plus two Marine tank companies, forced their way north to keep this road open, but suffered heavy losses at 'Hellfire Valley'.

The temperature regularly fell to below minus 10 degrees Fahrenheit

In spite of its difficulties this relieving force (known as Task Force Drysdale) enabled the forward Marine units to pull back towards Hagaru, and from an airstrip hacked out of the frozen ground, the wounded were flown out. By 6 December, Smith was able to move his men from Hagaru to Koto-ri, and to prepare for the next stage of the retreat – from Koto-ri to Chinhung-ni, via the Funchilin Bridge, which had been destroyed in the fighting. Covering the pass was Hill 1081, and the 1st Battalion of Puller's 1st Regiment took this feature in an epic night attack. By noon on 9 December the pass was secured, and a prefabricated bridge was flown in – an unprecedented engineering feat in the conditions.

This fighting was taking place in appalling weather. The temperature had dropped sharply on 10 November, regularly falling to below minus 10 degrees Fahrenheit, and the cold-weather clothing that had been distributed was ineffective against this kind of cold. On some nights, even the oil in the machine guns froze. Tank engines had to be kept

Above: A US Air Force Sikorsky R-5, equipped with externally mounted stretchers. The US Marines used helicopters to lift troops into combat for the first time in October 1951, during an advance towards the Soyang river. As early as September 1950, Marines had used helicopters for reconnaissance and for evacuating casualties, and at Inchon officers employed the Sikorsky HO3S-1 to give them a vantage point from which to observe several hundred yards of front. Later, when the front lines were more stable, the Marines found further uses for these new machines. By September 1951, whole companies were transported by air, mainly by Sikorsky HRS-1s, and soon whole battalions were being heli-lifted into combat. The US Army did not use helicopters on such a scale until rather later in the war.

Above: Marines and M47 Patton tanks south of Koto-ri during the retreat to Hungnam. It was necessary to fly a bridge in sections to the Marines at Koto-ri to enable them to break out.

running at regular intervals and contact with exposed metal could rip the skin off an ungloved hand.

Yet even in this terrible environment, the Marines, aware that they were at the end of a long vulnerable road, with an enormous enemy force massing around them, kept their order and fighting spirit. Air power was on their side, and during the day they could expect carrier-borne planes to cover them; resupply from the air, too, was invaluable. But in the end, the soldiers on the ground had to fight and march their way out of the jaws of a closing trap. This they did to great effect, for, after the Funchilin Pass, the Chinese were in no condition to put any further blocks on their progress. Indeed, Smith felt that he could maintain a perimeter around Hungnam, but Almond ordered him to evacuate all his forces. On 15 December the Marines sailed from Hungnam. Since landing at Wonsan, they had suffered over 4000 battle casualties, and over 7000 non-battle casualties, mainly caused by the cold. They estimated, however, that they had inflicted some 35,000 casualties on the Chinese forces.

The 1st Marine Division landed at Pusan, and soon refitted – by January it was operating again, rounding up guerrillas behind the front line. It played an important part during the advance north in the early spring, notably in the clearing of Chunchon at bayonet point; and then in blocking the main axis of the communist counter-offensive in the late spring. During the summer, the Division fought its way north to the 'Punchbowl' area, where the Marines distinguished themselves in a series of actions culminating in the Bloody Ridge battle. During the long stalemate that ensued, they maintained their sector of line against all enemy assaults, until the signing of the armistice on 27 July 1953. The Leathernecks had shown once again that they were an indispensable part of the US military establishment; and at Chosin they had demonstrated that they were not just a spearhead of assault – when they needed to, they could fight they way out of a hole with the sort of dogged determination that characterises a truly great fighting Corps.

2

WELCOME TO THE MARINES
Boot Camp Training

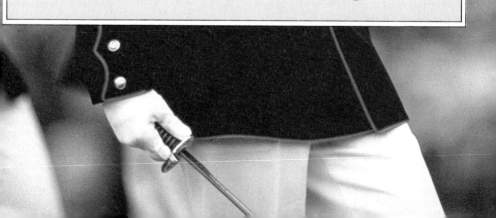

The author of this chapter, Dr V. Keith Fleming, passed through the Marine training camp at Parris Island in 1960. He was commissioned after three years' service, and served in Vietnam from 1966–67 as a captain and company commander. He has been appointed to edit the official history of Parris Island.

A recruit into the US Marine Corps will be sent to one of two depots for his basic training: Parris Island, South Carolina, or San Diego, California. The Parris Island recruit depot is on the site of the Port Royal Naval Station, which was guarded from its foundation in 1891 by a Marine detachment. A recruit depot was first set up in 1911 at Port Royal, but after two months it was transferred to Norfolk Navy Yard in Virginia. The recruit depot was moved back to the Marine Barracks in 1915, where it has remained ever since. The name of the base was changed to Parris Island in 1919. The Marines' association with San Diego began in 1914 when Marines set up a base known as Camp Howard, on an island in the vicinity. This was moved to the mainland later that year, but a permanent site was not fixed until 1919. The recruit depot was moved to San Diego from Mare Island in San Francisco Bay on 12 August 1923. The Marine Corps has usually relied on volunteers for its men, and has always applied strict regulations. Recruits are expected to be reasonably fit, to have a high-school diploma and to be US citizens. Recruits with a criminal record are rejected. Despite these high standards, the Corps has had some difficulties with its recruits, and the toughness of training has produced a high rate of desertion. But those who remained have fought hard when called upon to do so.

ASK ANY United States Marine what makes his Corps so special and he will probably answer, 'boot camp'. For the demanding, rugged, searing experience of Marine recruit training is the price of entry into that elite fraternity.

I started my Marine Corps service after I graduated from high school in 1960. The 'recruit experience' began for me and about 60 others on the bus ride from the recruiting station at Macon, Georgia. We were driving to the Marine Corps Recruit Depot at Parris Island, South Carolina. Our initially boisterous mood gradually died away as we approached the base. And once through the depot's gates, we recruits retreated into our own fears of the unknown.

Parris Island's geographical isolation contributed to our apprehension. En route, the bus had passed through many miles of flat, sandy, coastal Carolina, where huge oaks brooded over an occasional decaying shanty. Every large stream had wide desolate-looking salt marshes along its banks.

Parris Island lies between Charleston, South Carolina, and Savannah, Georgia. It is actually only a piece of slightly higher ground amid the salt marshes lining Port Royal Sound. Channels meandering through the marshes separate it from other spots of high ground. In the not-too-distant past, recruits like ourselves had reached the recruit depot by boat from Port Royal. Even now, one felt far from civilisation. Only a few distant lights across the marshes hinted to us that other people inhabited the region.

In summer, Parris Island is as hot and heavily humid as any tropical rain forest; only the frequent thunderstorms break the mugginess. Winters are also damp, but seldom cold enough to interfere with training. For us during that long, hot summer, however, the coolness of winter was only a dream.

The next morning our DIs arrived. Then the shock treatment began

At the receiving barracks, a khaki-clad sergeant entered the bus and brusquely ordered us inside the building. It was already after dark, but there were forms for us to complete before going to bed. The next morning we had breakfast and then sat quietly – at a sergeant's orders – until our drill instructors (always known as 'DIs') arrived. Then, the shock treatment began.

We new recruits did not realise it, but DIs take command of a brand new platoon by staging a ritual as repetitive as the nightly performances of a play in the theatre. And just as in the theatre, each performance and the individual interpretations of a role can vary. DIs judge each others' performance at platoon 'pick-up' as critically as do actors, and praise from his peers establishes a DI's reputation.

The senior DI plays the leading role in every new performance while his junior DIs comprise the supporting cast. Their costumes are the normal service uniforms with the significant addition of the peaked hat that serves as their badge of office. The script carries a new platoon through the

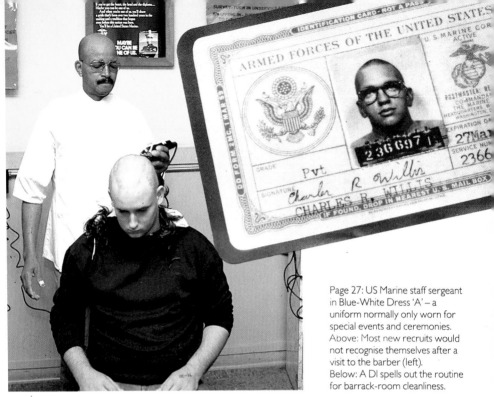

Page 27: US Marine staff sergeant in Blue-White Dress 'A' – a uniform normally only worn for special events and ceremonies.
Above: Most new recruits would not recognise themselves after a visit to the barber (left).
Below: A DI spells out the routine for barrack-room cleanliness.

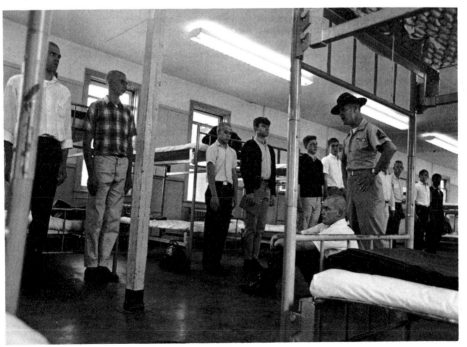

Welcome to the Marines

Right: A staff sergeant examines new recruits' personal effects. Alcoholic drink, lethal weapons, books, radios and similar items are not permitted to 'boots'.

Below: A DI inspects a group of 'boots' wearing silver training helmets.

Right: As part of their indoctrination, and with the object of instilling an *esprit de corps*, 'boots' are made to crawl through a sand ditch while singing 'I love the Marine Corps.'

Above: A platoon of 'boots' returns from a run. The early stages of the training programme are intended to build up physical strength and stamina.

first few hectic days of recruit training. The purpose of all this play-acting is ruthlessly simple: to strip away the recruits' civilian attitudes and reduce all platoon members to the same level as quickly as possible.

Scene one opens at the receiving barracks: shouting DIs make the recruits (now known as 'boots') run outside and stand to attention in rough semblance of a military formation. The DIs ceaselessly stalk about the platoon, their anger ready to boil over at any moment. They shout or scream in ways and words most of the young privates have never heard before – and certainly not at such close quarters. For the DIs even invade the several square feet of 'personal space' that surround most people. We get uncomfortable when strangers or mere acquaintances move into that space. The DIs, however, deliberately establish their domination by entering the recruits' personal space to engage literally in face-to-face, even nose-to-nose, confrontations. Startled young men who cannot maintain the 'eyes front' positions of 'attention' and glance at a DI, suddenly find their very manhood called into question as the DI sneeringly demands if the recruit is a homosexual with a passion for the DI. By this time, the recruits have become frightened and confused; they do not comprehend the questions nor know the answers.

To the new recruits the DIs sound like insane, violent sadists

Soon the whole civilian frame of reference of the recruits begins to shatter under a concerted onslaught. The outward signs of status among civilian American males appear in their hair styles and clothing; so the Marines first shave off the hair. The recruits hardly recognise themselves, much less each other. Then, still enduring the DI's constant harangues, they pack their civilian clothes for shipment home. Disorientated, shaven-headed, and dressed in wrinkled new field uniforms, the recruits have no idea of how to act properly, speak or think in their strange new environment. For a day or so, the system isolates them from practically every influence except that of the screaming drill instructors.

The DIs do not let up with their eyeball-to-eyeball harangues as they begin their elementary instruction. The repetition of basic military movements continues until the recruits get them right. To the new recruits the DIs continue to sound like insane, violent sadists totally devoid of humanity. Nevertheless, the DIs are imparting new knowledge, and making it become second nature to the former civilians. The lessons continue until lights out, and even in sleep some of the recruits will be unable to escape their new environment: a few will wake during the night with muscle cramps from sleeping at rigid attention.

This introduction to the Marine Corps sends many young men into a terrified, bewildered state, close to shock. But human beings are adaptable creatures, and new recruits quickly learn the rules of the new society. They begin

Left, top to bottom: 'Boots' practise their 'war faces' during training. Shouting and grimacing stimulate the aggressive feelings that are a part of the Corps ethos.

33

Far right (main picture): A close-combat instructor shows a recruit the right way to tackle the enemy. Far right (inset): A Marine wearing the protective equipment for combat with pugil sticks. These are wooden sticks with padded ends which are used to train Marines in close combat. This protection is necessary for the pugil sticks have proved to be fatal to recruits when used inappropriately.

emulating the DIs, as much as their limited knowledge permits. The training system has begun to shape them.

The training system usually identifies problem 'boots' within the first day of training. For example, each platoon takes an initial physical fitness test, to measure the trainees' ability at pushups, situps, squat thrusts, and running. A few men fail this test due to lack of strength or stamina, or because of obesity. Those who fail go to the special training unit's strength platoon, which uses diet and exercises to improve fitness. A weight-control platoon uses a similar approach, but gears it to the special needs of overweight recruits. When men assigned to either platoon finally pass the initial strength test, they join a platoon just entering training.

In my year, not all recruits responded to the DIs' well-polished methods. Some, who simply would not give a maximum effort in training, were assigned to the motivation platoon. This platoon had two separate programmes for straightening out young men's attitudes. A one-day motivation programme worked for those who needed encouragement to give just a little more effort. Those recruits not amenable to the one-day programme became full-time members of the motivation platoon. There they received professional psychiatric evaluation and counselling, training in normal military subjects, and a good dose of physical exercise. Some had to sit in front of a large mirror for several hours of self-examination in which, hopefully, they would sort out their attitudes towards the training and the Marine Corps. They even viewed inspirational movies such as John Wayne's *Sands of Iwo Jima* as a means of increasing their self-identification with the Marine Corps.

Rigorous daily exercise quickly improved our physical fitness

The 'shock treatment' marked the beginning of the first of the three phases that have always characterised Marine Corps recruit training. This first phase is an intense introduction to the basic fundamentals of military life. Emphasis has always been on discipline, with close order drill under arms serving as the primary teaching tool. My platoon, like all others, learned to march smartly with and without our M1 rifles, to salute, to take care of our weapons, and to master a variety of similar military skills. Long hours marching on the huge asphalt parade ground (the 'grinder') and rigorous daily exercise quickly improved our physical fitness.

The second phase, marksmanship training, took place at the rifle range. It was, in many ways, the most relaxed period of recruit training. The DIs, of course, never stopped demanding excellence. They did, however, ease up on the personal pressure that kept us recruits off-balance. They did so because marksmanship requires a calm approach.

We spent the first week at the range learning to coax our bodies into the proper firing positions. During this time, trained marksmanship coaches taught us the techniques of

A crucial aspect of Marine training is marksmanship and maintenance of personal smallarms. Many hours are spent on the ranges to familiarise the men with the service rifle and the various firing positions and techniques before the recruit becomes qualified, and earns the right to wear the Rifle Expert decoration (shown above) on the left breast-pocket of his uniform. But while accuracy of shooting is heavily emphasised, recruits must also become totally at home with the weapon and its working. Step-by-step drills for field stripping the M14 and M16 rifles are clearly laid out in the Marine service manuals and must become second nature to the new soldier. Proper care of the weapon will prevent most stoppages and mechanical malfunctions, and considerable time is spent on cleaning and lubricating procedures. When a weapon does jam, the recruit must be able to identify immediately which of the main categories of stoppage has occurred and apply the standard corrective measures. All procedures must be executed in the correct order and are drilled into the men until they know them by heart; for in combat, precious seconds wasted in fumbling with the mechanism of a jammed rifle can mean the difference between life and death.

Left: A Marine takes aim on the firing range with an M16A1.
Below: A 'boot' is shown by a DI the correct firing position.

using and adjusting the rifle's sights and the proper trigger squeeze. Repetition, the key to so much Marine recruit training, gave us mastery of the subject. The platoon's members spent hours in the various firing positions, practising lining up their sights on a target and then squeezing the triggers of their empty M1 rifles. The marksmanship coaches emphasised the importance of accurate shooting. They reminded us that noise on the battlefield kills no enemy. Hitting the enemy with properly aimed fire is all that counts.

The second week of marksmanship training gave us the chance to fire live ammunition for the first time. We began on the pistol range with .22in target rifles and pistols. Later in the week we fired the .45in M1911A1 pistol, to get us familiar with this standard weapon. Each afternoon, however, we fired our M1 rifles on the regular ranges. The first few afternoons enabled us to determine the elevation and windage required on our sights to hit the target at ranges of 200, 300, and 500yd. We also grew familiar with the qualification course and with the noise and recoil of our rifles. By the end of the week the coaches and DIs knew how well each recruit was firing, and those with low scores began receiving extra instruction.

Failure to qualify with the rifle could bring a recruit trouble

The goal of the third week at the range was to qualify the recruits with their rifles on the Friday morning. There were three categories of qualified riflemen. Out of a possible 250 points (five points for each of the 50 rounds fired), a man needed 190 to be a 'marksman', 210 for 'sharpshooter', and 220 for 'expert'. Failure to post a qualifying score with the rifle could bring a recruit trouble from his fellow recruits as well as the DIs. After a platoon finished its firing on Friday morning, some DIs made the non-qualifiers wear their shooting jackets backwards. These forlorn recruits marched at the rear of their platoons with their rifles carried upside down. Successful recruits felt that non-qualifiers had let down the team.

Condemnation from the DIs was to be expected, but that from the rest of the platoon reflected one of the major changes the 'boots' underwent at the range. We began looking outside the narrow confines of our own platoon and realised there were three other platoons with whom we were competing. Our platoon of about 75 men was part of a series of four such consecutively numbered units under the command of a first lieutenant. The DIs had told us before qualification day that one platoon would be the honor platoon on graduation day. Our qualification percentage on the rifle range, they said, would play a major role in determining which platoon received that recognition. Unit loyalty and pride fuelled a new-found competitive spirit among us.

Following the marksmanship phase, a platoon normally spent a week assigned to either mess or maintenance duty.

The latter included projects such as cutting grass, trimming
hedges, raking leaves, or painting rocks to keep the depot a
show place for the Corps. Mess duty meant working long
hours in the mess halls assisting the cooks, washing pots and
pans, sweeping and mopping floors, and serving food on the
mess line.

The third, and final phase of basic training involved
putting some polish on the recruit platoons. During this
phase, the DIs coaxed maximum effort from the 'boots' by
encouraging intense competition among us. The recruits
responded readily – each wanted his unit to be the series
honor platoon.

The increasing tempo of training reinforced our growing
pride and spirit. We had our day on the Confidence Course, a
special obstacle course requiring strength, agility and a
degree of physical courage. On another day, tailors fitted the
platoon's newly issued summer and winter service uniforms.
Even the receipt of our metal identification tags ('dog tags')
added to our perception of our growing seniority.

Above: Marines attempt to fix their position during a navigation exercise in the Appalachian Mountains.

Left: A Marine Corps corporal in Dress Blue 'B' uniform. The two ribbons on his left breast indicate a meritorious unit citation (green and yellow stripes – with a star for a second award) and the Marine good conduct medal (red-blue-red bands). Below them are worn the Marine Rifle Expert badge (with two bars for further awards) and pistol sharpshooter badge. The 'blood' stripe on the trouser seams distinguishes NCOs, warrant officers and officers from enlisted men.

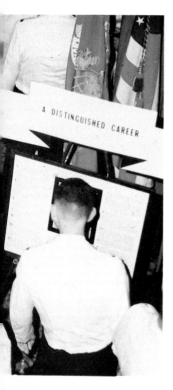

Above: Marine officers wear formal dress for a special occasion. Since the 1950s elaborate ceremony has become a part of Marine tradition.

My luck ran out at this point. During physical training one day, I did not do enough satisfactory pushups. The PT instructor put me to lifting weights to increase my upper-body strength. Unfortunately, in lowering the weights, I brought them down behind my head and dislocated my left shoulder. The problem was correctly diagnosed as a condition existing prior to my enlistment, and I quickly received a medical discharge from the Marine Corps.

The medical discharge put me in the '4-F' draft category and thus exempt from further military service. However, I didn't want to be a civilian. I wanted to be a Marine – and the Marine Corps gave me a second chance. After surgery at my own expense, the Corps waived my discharge the following year and again enlisted me as a private.

The Marines sent me back to Parris Island to repeat the whole recruit experience from beginning to end. Of course, I had advantages over my fellow recruits. Not the least of these was that my DIs took care of me despite some remaining weaknesses in my shoulder. They believed that anyone who wanted to be a Marine strongly enough to go through Parris Island twice deserved to graduate, despite mediocre performance at pushups and chinups. My new training was exactly as it had been the year before. Not until my new platoon entered the last phase of training did I encounter anything new.

The final days of recruit training were long and hectic

The final days of recruit training were long and hectic as we prepared for and passed a series of tests. These included written examinations on academic knowledge, a final physical fitness test, and the series drill competition. The judges in the latter were very senior NCOs, all of whom wore the DI's peaked field hat. A platoon's close order drill had to be exceptional to win the competition.

The last major hurdle for every platoon was the 'Final Field Inspection', conducted by a team of officers and senior NCOs from the recruit training battalion. In preparation, the DIs had us recruits strip down our rifles and meticulously remove any speck of old grease, dirt and carbon. On the night before the inspection the DIs wore white gloves to check every weapon. The platoon then stacked the rifles carefully and covered them with clean white bed sheets. We completed our preparations by spit-shining our dress shoes, polishing brass belt buckles, and carefully clipping any remaining loose threads from our service uniforms.

The next morning, the platoon dressed with great care to avoid wrinkling its service uniforms. When we formed up outside we stepped cautiously to avoid scuffing or kicking sand or dust on our gleaming shoes. One recruit stood by the barracks door going over the rifles with a vacuum cleaner brought from home by a DI. The inspection itself went quickly, for the inspecting officers had performed this ritual many times. This was the final test before graduation.

At one time recruits simply completed their training, packed their gear in a seabag, and joined an operating unit. Since the 1950s, however, recruit graduations have been major events. Elaborate ceremonies, to which recruits invite family and friends, deliberately add significance to the formal bestowing of the title 'Marine'.

On graduation day, I received, probably because of my greater experience as a recruit, a promotion to private, 1st class. That made me happy, but nothing compared to the surge of pride that came while standing in ranks on the parade ground while the depot band played the Marines' hymn. I had made it; I was a Marine!

In 1967, after commanding an infantry company in Vietnam as a captain, I joined the Recruit Training Regiment at San Diego, California. Other than being compressed into eight weeks rather than the 11 or 12 of the pre-war years, the training at boot camp had changed little. The DIs remained the key players in the process of transforming young men into Marines. Of course, more men were in training and some

Below: At the end of all the training, the Marines must be ready to go into action. These Marines are landing at Da Nang in 1965. The operational performance of the Marines in Vietnam demonstrated the effectiveness of their training.

Welcome to the Marines

Below: Recruit Private R. A. Keller as he appeared at the receiving barracks, and again (bottom) three months later, on graduation from recruit training.

of them had to live in tents. The Corps had shortened marksmanship training from three to two weeks. Recruits began firing their service rifles during the first week and qualified on the Friday of the second week. The rifle in use had also changed, from the old M1 to the M14 (Marines in Vietnam had recently received the M16A1 rifle).

During the Vietnam War, the two recruit depots ran their recruit graduation ceremonies differently, yet both sought to provide a show-piece for the recruits' guests. San Diego's graduations began in the depot theatre and resembled a traditional school graduation. Afterwards, a truncated version of a military parade concluded the ceremony outside. Parris Island, on the other hand, conducted a full-scale military parade. Both depots' ceremonies included congratulatory speeches from the battalion commander and the promotion of outstanding recruits to private, 1st class. The top man in each platoon received the Marines' blue dress uniform. Each ceremony concluded with the graduates being addressed as 'Marines' for the very first time. The DIs then dismissed their platoons, which invariably let out a loud cheer, and the new Marines went looking for their families and friends in the audience. This was a moment that always brought grins to the faces of veteran Marines. Parents and friends often barely recognised the young man they had come to see; some of the young Marines had grown taller, others had developed new muscles or deep tans. All had changed, all had become Marines.

The next day, the graduates left the depot for further training. Boot camp had made them basic Marines but they were not yet ready for combat. Prior to the Vietnam War, all Marines received four weeks of infantry training at either Camp Lejeune, North Carolina, or Camp Pendleton, California. During the war, only those with infantry-related specialities took the full course. The rest received their requisite combat training during their basic specialist training courses or at the replacement battalion before going to Vietnam. Today, the course at boot camp includes a block of combat training adequate for all but infantrymen.

The development of an *esprit de corps* through a demanding initiation rite is the fundamental reason why the Marines keep their recruit training so intense. Boot camp serves the Marine Corps as the academies serve the other armed services. It is the fountainhead of the Corps' eliteness. The training itself is on a very basic level and could be taught in a far more benign environment, while all recruit graduates require further training before joining the operating forces. Boot camp, however, gives all Marines – whether infantrymen, truck drivers, aircraft mechanics, or computer operators – a common background with which they all identify.

Back at the recruit depots, after the graduation ceremonies, the new Marines who disperse to celebrate with families and friends will never be the same again; boot camp transforms them. For the rest of their lives they will know they are members of that elite fraternity, the US Marine Corps.

3

UNDER SIEGE
The Battle of Khe Sanh

CAPTAIN WILLIAM DABNEY

The author of this chapter,
Captain William Dabney,
commanded India Company on
Hill 881S during the battle of Khe
Sanh. The combat base was
strategically sited on a plateau
dominated by a line of hills to the
north. The US military command
in Vietnam feared that if these hills
fell into North Vietnamese hands
Khe Sanh would be made
untenable by enemy artillery.
Colonel Lownds, the commander
at Khe Sanh, placed most of his
infantry on these hills, where they
fended off many infantry assaults
during the 77-day battle. The
combat base itself was brought
under heavy fire from 21 January
1968 onward. The enemy also
dug earthworks to approach the
perimeter and launched a major
attack on 29 February that was
beaten off in heavy fighting. In
March a relief column for Khe
Sanh was organised by the US
forces in Vietnam. Troops of the
1st Cavalry Division (Airmobile)
provided a helicopter-borne
assault force, while men of the 1st
Marines advanced along Route 9.
The relief operation, codenamed
Pegasus, began on 1 April, and the
base was reached six days later.
President Johnson hailed the battle
of Khe Sanh as a decisive victory.

THE SNIPER was well concealed on a hill about 400yd to the north, the only hill high enough and close enough to our positions on Hill 881 South to offer a vantage point for effective rifle fire. He had been there about a week. He fired only rarely, when visibility was good and a clear target was offered, and he was deadly. With a total of perhaps 20 rounds, he had killed two Marines and wounded half-a-dozen others. He was patient, waiting for an artillery mission that would force the gunners into the open, or a 'medevac' helicopter mission to evacuate wounded – the stretcher bearers made easy targets as they stumbled across the rough landing zone to the chopper with their burdens – and he was careful. On the one day that was not overcast, we had directed napalm strikes to blanket the area where we knew he must be, but the next cloudy day he was back, and still deadly. He knew very well that our jets could not be used so close to friendly lines through clouds.

But he was not careful enough. On a still afternoon, a machine-gunner, one of a dozen Marines who patiently kept watch on the hillside, saw a slight movement in a bush. We had reckoned that the sniper had a hole, and was well protected from smallarms fire, and so the gunner fired to pin him in the hole, while he called for something heavier. A 106mm recoilless rifle, our primary mid-range anti-tank gun, was brought laboriously along the trench from the south side of the hill (where it covered the only feasible tank approach to our position) and sighted onto the gunner's target. Following his precise directions, a high-explosive plastic round, designed to blow a track or turret from a tank, crashed through the bush, making a crater of the hole and formless pulp of its occupant.

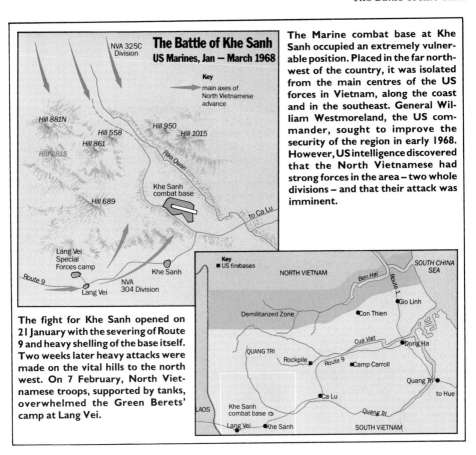

The Battle of Khe Sanh
US Marines, Jan — March 1968

Key
→ main axes of North Vietnamese advance

NVA 325C Division

Hill 881N
Hill 558
Hill 861
Hill 881S
Hill 950
Hill 1015
Rao Quan
Hill 689
Khe Sanh combat base
to Ca Lu
Lang Vei Special Forces camp
Route 9
Khe Sanh
Lang Vei
NVA 304 Division

The Marine combat base at Khe Sanh occupied an extremely vulnerable position. Placed in the far northwest of the country, it was isolated from the main centres of the US forces in Vietnam, along the coast and in the southeast. General William Westmoreland, the US commander, sought to improve the security of the region in early 1968. However, US intelligence discovered that the North Vietnamese had strong forces in the area – two whole divisions – and that their attack was imminent.

Key
■ US firebases

NORTH VIETNAM
SOUTH CHINA SEA
Ben Hai
Route 1
Gio Linh
Demilitarized Zone
Con Thien
Cua Viet
Dong Ha
QUANG TRI
Rockpile
Route 9
Camp Carroll
Quang Tri
LAOS
Ca Lu
to Hue
Khe Sanh combat base
Quang Tri
Lang Vei   Khe Sanh
SOUTH VIETNAM

The fight for Khe Sanh opened on 21 January with the severing of Route 9 and heavy shelling of the base itself. Two weeks later heavy attacks were made on the vital hills to the north west. On 7 February, North Vietnamese troops, supported by tanks, overwhelmed the Green Berets' camp at Lang Vei.

The sniper's hill was too far away for us to maintain an outpost on it safely, and since the North Vietnamese could move with relative impunity at night and in fog, he was soon replaced. Over the next 10 days, this second sniper killed one and wounded several other Marines. Inevitably, he too was spotted. Again the 106, a crater, and a pulpy mess.

We settled in to wait. It was a short wait, for within two days, the sniping began again. By now, the artillerymen and stretcher bearers were very worried. Any exposure for more than a few seconds invited the sharp crack of a rifle round. It was especially bad during the medevacs, because the crack of the bullet going by would cause the stretcher bearers to hit the deck, dropping their wounded comrade with an agonising jar. But the new sniper was soon located, and the crew again wrestled the 106 around the hill. As its gunner patiently adjusted it onto the point described by the spotter, a young private approached me. Crouched in the trench, he observed that this third sniper had been in position a week, had fired about as many rounds as his predecessors, but hadn't hit a damned thing. He suggested

Page 43: Marines on the main base at Khe Sanh dive for cover as yet another North Vietnamese artillery barrage crashes down. Far left: The control tower on Khe Sanh airstrip. During the 77-day siege, the air controllers guided in 455 aircraft, often under heavy artillery fire.

STOPPED BY A BULLET

'It is night and the sky is burning with slowly dropping magnesium flares. Heaps of equipment are on fire, terrifying in their jagged black massiveness, burning prehistoric shapes like the tail of a C-130 sticking straight up in the air, dead metal showing through the grey-black smoke. God, if it can do that to metal, what will it do to me? And then something very near me is smouldering, just above my head, the damp canvas coverings on the sandbags lining the top of a slit trench. It is a small trench, and a lot of us have gotten into it in a hurry. At the end farthest from me there is a young guy who has been hit in the throat, and he is making the sounds a baby will make when he is trying to work up the breath for a good scream. We were on the ground when those rounds came, and a Marine nearer the trench had been splattered badly across the legs and groin. I sort of took him into the trench with me and he kept swearing and shouting until someone told him that I wasn't a grunt but a reporter. Then he started to say, very quietly, 'Be careful, Mister. Please be careful.' He'd been wounded before, and he knew how it would hurt in a few minutes. Far up the road that skirted the TOC (tactical operations centre) was a dump where they burned the gear and uniforms that nobody needed any more. On top of the pile I saw a flak jacket so torn apart that no one would ever want it again. On the back, its owner had listed the months that he had served in Vietnam. *March, April, May* (each month written out in a tentative, spidery hand), *June, July, August, September, Octobler, Novembler, Decembler, Janurary, Feburary*, the list ending right there like a clock stopped by a bullet.'
Michael Herr, freelance journalist, Khe Sanh.

that we leave him be, for if we blew him away, the North Vietnamese would surely replace him, and his successor might be better. This idea made sense, and the 106 was moved back.

For a time, the Marines amused themselves by waving 'Maggie's drawers' – a red cloth that is the traditional signal for a miss on the rifle range – every time the sniper fired, but it

Far left: Another Marine casualty from the front line is carried to a landing zone to be flown out by helicopter.
Below: Marines on Hill 881S manhandle a 106mm recoilless rifle to a new position. This gun was used to knock out enemy snipers deeply dug in on the opposite hillside.

eventually occurred to us that this sniper was perhaps not so poor a marksman as he was crafty. He knew the fate of his predecessors, and would logically do whatever he could to avoid it. He had to fire regularly to satisfy his superiors, but since they could never determine whether he hit or not, his most sensible course was to miss deliberately, keeping his officers happy without provoking our response. So to support what we assumed to be his ruse, we quit taunting him, and sometimes even faked casualties. He stayed there for the remainder of the battle – about two months – fired regularly, and never hit a man.

Hill 881 South (881S) was one of several high hills overlooking Khe Sanh Combat Base, the remote Marine regiment outpost in the northwest corner of South Vietnam that came under attack from two divisions of North Vietnamese in early 1968. The Marines at Khe Sanh had made a detailed study of the battle for Dien Bien Phu where the French forces in Indochina had suffered a devastating defeat in 1954 at the hands of the Viet Minh. The French had made the grave mistake of allowing the Viet Minh to bring up massive quantities of artillery, that wreaked havoc on the French defences, and the Marines recognised that denial of the hills surrounding Khe Sanh to the enemy was crucial to a successful defence of the low-lying base.

Not all of the hills offered defensible terrain, but there were sufficient to enable us to engage the enemy and to provide observation positions for the Marines over the likely North Vietnamese routes of advance on the base from their staging areas to the west in Laos. None was more critical, nor more exposed, than 881S, a steep-sided hill rising 1500ft from its surrounding valleys, some 5 miles west of the base. It had been the scene of a bloody fight a year before, when the North Vietnamese holding it had chosen, uncharacteristically for that time in the war, to stand and fight. The attacking Marines had finally seized it after several costly assaults, and the massive bombing and artillery barrages that helped them carry it had left its slopes devoid of vegetation, pocked with craters, and littered with collapsed bunkers in which the remains of North Vietnamese soldiers were still entombed.

This was 'Indian Country', crawling with enemy troops

The hill overlooked Route 9, the old French highway that wound its way west from Khe Sanh across the Laotian border to Tchepone. This was 'Indian Country', in the parlance of the young Marines at Khe Sanh, and crawling with enemy troops.

There was also a road running east from the base to the Marine coastal bastions near the Demilitarized Zone; but this route twisted for 15 miles through narrow gorges and across several bridges and the North Vietnamese Army (NVA) had closed it several months earlier. All supplies for both the main base and the hill positions had to be brought in by air. The base had a runway of steel matting, and for a time, even

US MARINES IN VIETNAM

US Marine involvement in Vietnam began in 1954 when a small advisory group arrived to work with the South Vietnamese Marine Corps. US concern over the situation in Southeast Asia mounted in the early 1960s and a helicopter squadron was deployed to Vietnam in 1962 to assist South Vietnamese troops fighting the Viet Cong. Over the next three years, individual Marine squadrons were rotated for six-month tours.

However, in February 1965 President Lyndon Johnson decided to commit ground troops to Vietnam; elements of the 3rd Marine Division landed at Da Nang in March. By August four Marine Regiments, supported by four Marine Air Groups, were operating in Vietnam and their first major operation – Starlite – was launched. More Marine units arrived throughout 1965 and 1966, including the 26th Marines, defenders of Khe Sanh. The introduction of the Vietnamization policy in late 1967 reduced the need for US combat troops and large-scale troop withdrawals were begun after the defeat of the Tet Offensive of 1968. On 25 June 1971, the last Marine combat troops were withdrawn from Vietnam.

Left: US Marines patrolling on a hill post.

after the so-called 'siege' had begun, four-engined C-130 cargo planes landed regularly with supplies. After NVA anti-aircraft fire had become too intense to permit such landings, the base had to be resupplied by paradrops. Water was available from streams and a well at the base.

The surrounding occupied hills, however, with their small perimeters, could be served only by helicopter, and constant resupply was necessary, for the Marines held only the crests, which meant that they had no access to fresh water. To send a water party down the exposed slopes to the nearest streams was to invite a major skirmish with the surrounding North Vietnamese. If the water party suffered casualties – which it almost certainly would – it required reinforcement to fight its way back up the hill with its wounded, and the only source of reinforcement available was the unit holding the top of the hill; this, in turn, meant denuding the defences, and as the prime mission of these units was to hold their assigned hills, getting to water was too much of a risk to contemplate.

In any case, it was not tactically sensible to engage in firefights lower down the slopes, since the Marines' main advantage lay in their occupation of fixed positions with everything around them a 'free-fire' zone. With virtually unlimited artillery and air support available, it was unnecessary to manoeuvre on the ground to dispose of enemy formations, and to do so only complicated the coordination of supporting arms. The simple, and ultimately successful, tactic was to stay on the hills, whose locations were well-known to the artillerymen and aviators, and direct massive fire, using everything from B-52 strategic bombers to 60mm mortars, and, close in, machine guns and hand grenades, to attack every possible observed or suspected enemy position and formation.

Hill 881S was the most distant and difficult to reinforce

Each hill was held by a company-sized unit, all part of or attached to the 26th Marine Regiment that had overall responsibility for the defence of Khe Sanh. Hill 881S, being the most distant and most difficult to reinforce, had all of Company I ('India') and two platoons and the headquarters of Company M ('Mike'), 3rd Battalion, 26th Marines. With a section of 81mm mortars (2 tubes), 106mm recoilless rifles (2 guns), and a detachment of 105mm howitzers (3 guns), on 20 January 1968, the defenders under my command totalled some 400 Marines.

Intelligence had accurately predicted the NVA's intention to besiege or attack Khe Sanh, and three battalions of about 1000 Marines each had been flown to the base during December and January to reinforce the battalion already in place. With a 300-man battalion of South Vietnamese Rangers and normal supporting units, the garrison totalled about 6000 men, deployed on the base itself and in the surrounding hills.

Although there had been no major engagements before 20 January, we had been patrolling aggressively around 881S, and, on the 18th and 19th, had fought skirmishes with North Vietnamese soldiers to the north of the hill, where patrols had previously passed unmolested. Concerned about an enemy build-up to the north, I sought permission to take India Company out on a reconnaissance-in-force to determine the North Vietnamese dispositions and, if possible, disrupt them.

The company jumped off before dawn on the 20th, moving cautiously through thick vegetation, and had advanced barely 500yd when its two lead platoons, moving in mutually supporting columns about 400yd apart, were hit by heavy fire from a substantial enemy force. The right platoon, under Lieutenant Richard Fromme, held fast on good ground, but, with several serious casualties to take care of, it had to secure

Below: Hill posts, such as the one on 881S, were subjected to probing attacks by the North Vietnamese which often resulted in close-quarters fighting. The Marines holding 881S suffered heavy casualties during these attacks, sometimes as many as 50 per cent of their personnel. Far left: Marines defending a hill post call in a helicopter to evacuate casualties.

Above: Marine engineers repair the airstrip at Khe Sanh.

a landing zone to evacuate the wounded before it could move on. As the medevac helicopter came into Fromme's zone, it was hit by machine-gun fire and sheared away to crash-land in a nearby gully. Marines from Lieutenant Michael Thomas' reserve platoon, which had been following in Fromme's footsteps and who were securing the zone, jumped unordered from their positions and made a lightning dash 200yd down the hill to the crash site. Their charge was so sudden and unexpected that a startled group of North Vietnamese soldiers, hidden in the savannah grass between the landing zone and the crash site, leaped to their feet and ran headlong out of sight without firing a shot.

The Marines quickly pulled out the injured helicopter crewmen and returned to the zone, which Thomas then moved to a better covered position behind the hill. The wounded were then safely lifted out by another helicopter.

While the right flank was fully occupied with these events, Lieutenant Thomas Brindley's platoon on the left found itself pinned down on exposed ground, about 200yd short of a commanding knoll from which the North Vietnamese were firing with telling effect. Brindley, a man who was by nature not inclined to retreat, realised that he could not hold his present position without support, and so directed several barrages of artillery at the knoll. Moving his Marines into position under cover of the shellfire, he then launched a classic infantry assault and stormed the hill. It was not without cost. Brindley was killed as he reached the crest, and with numerous other casualties, the platoon found itself holding the piece of high ground with depleted ammunition stocks

and only a lance-corporal in command.

An enemy skirmish line then charged up the rear slope to retake the hill but was annihilated by a napalm drop so close to the Marines' lines that several soldiers had their eyebrows singed. The situation, however, was still desperate, and, with Fromme holding on the right, I took Thomas' reserve platoon across the intervening gully to relieve the Marines on the knoll and move the wounded back for medevac.

I soon discovered that an eight-man reconnaissance team attached to Brindley's platoon had become disorientated during the assault and had strayed off into a gully to the left, where it was pinned down and under attack by enemy soldiers withdrawing from Brindley's hill. Thomas, in a move typical of his aggressive brand of leadership, volunteered to

Below: A blazing aeroplane, set alight by shellfire, is extinguished by Marines.
Bottom: When landing aircraft became difficult due to artillery barrages, aerial resupply by parachute was adopted. Supplies were lashed to a wooden pallet and dropped from Hercules C-130s.

Under Siege

Below: A photographic map of Khe Sanh combat base. Several assaults were made against the main base but none ever seriously breached the perimeter.

find them and lead them back to the lines. He got about 20yd before he was felled by an enemy bullet. His platoon sergeant, David Jessup, immediately replaced him, located the team, and after several trips carrying wounded Marines, had them all back to relative safety.

By now, with the enemy forces located, India was bringing heavy supporting fire to bear, but, with darkness

Khe Sanh Combat Base

SUPPLY DROP ZONE

RED SECTOR

to Khe Sanh village

4.2in mortar bty

155mm howitzer bty

105mm howitzer bty

BLUE SECTOR

GREY SECTOR

Marine air traffic control unit

control tower

fire support coordination centre and 26th Marines command post

water point

main ammo dump

airstrip

105mm howitzer btys

main perimeter

approaching and its mission still the defence of 881S, it could advance no further. Under cover of artillery fire, the withdrawal was uneventful, and Company India rejoined Company Mike on the hill as darkness fell, weaker by 50 Marines than it had been that morning.

At about 0200 hours the following day, the North Vietnamese simultaneously assaulted several of the outlying positions with massed infantry. The lightly manned position at Khe Sanh village, a few hundred yards outside the base perimeter, had to be evacuated but the others repulsed the assaults, and constant artillery concentrations on North Vietnamese reserve staging areas and approach routes prevented their exploitation of their initial successes. Hill 881S, the most vulnerable position, was not assaulted, probably because India's fighting reconnaissance the previous day had revealed the NVA force moving into position against it, and had hurt it enough to discourage the attempt.

My mortarmen fired nearly 700 rounds at near-maximum range

During the battle of the 21st my 81mm mortarmen had fired nearly 700 rounds at near-maximum range from their two tubes to seal off the breach in the perimeter of Hill 861, our neighbouring position 2 miles to the northeast. The mortar tubes got so hot that the propellant ignited as the rounds slid down the tubes, causing the bombs to go unpredictably astray, and the tubes had to be cooled. The Marines used their precious water, but soon exhausted that and a meagre

Below: A group of Marines huddle in a trench during an enemy mortar barrage.

SHOWING THE FLAG

An extract from the Dallas *Time-Herald* of February 1968 provides an indication of the high morale on Hill 881 S: 'The flag is battered, heads are bloody, but "the colors" still sound on Hill 881. A tough Marine company led by Capt. William H. Dabney is today showing the Viet Cong how American fighting men respond to the rigors of the battle in the much beleaguered Khe Sanh combat complex. Each day, a torn and bullet riddled flag is hauled up an improvised flag pole on Hill 881, and then the muted tones of a bugle sounding "to the colors" echoes through the trenches and earthworks, Captain Dabney and his men stand at attention during the brief ceremonies, although enemy guns are trained on them every moment. They hit the dirt as soon as the last note is sounded.

India Company now has the unique position of performing the "most dangerous flag-raising ceremony in the world", according to reports from the battle zone.'

Above right: Under constant threat of mortar fire, a working-party of Marines extends the slit trench earthworks along the crest of a hill post.

Far right: A Marine prepares 60mm mortar shells for a fire mission.

cache of canned fruit juice. Finally, a 'daisy chain' of Marines was formed to urinate on the tubes.

With the opening round over, the units on the hill positions settled in for a prolonged contest. It began in earnest the next morning, on the 22nd, when, shortly after dawn, the main base was struck by several hundred rounds of large-calibre rocket and artillery fire, creating havoc along the runway and exploding the main ammunition dump. The shells came from two sources. The first was the line of deadly accurate artillery pieces – 152mm howitzer and 130mm guns – positioned in Laos to the west and southwest of the base. The second source, far greater in volume, consisted of sheaves of 122mm Russian-made rockets, fired 30 to 50 at a time from several positions at once, that had a devastating effect upon a target as large as Khe Sanh.

Having lost the element of surprise on 881S when we attacked north on the 20th, and faced thereafter with alert and well-emplaced defenders, ready to throw back a ground assault, the North Vietnamese decided to force us off the hill by cutting off our resupply. And had it not been for the unique structure of the Marine Air–Ground Team, they might have succeeded.

The mortars were impervious to anything short of a direct hit

The NVA began by positioning their 120mm mortars about 5000yd west of the hill, emplaced deep in the ground with narrow tunnels dug at the proper angle for the rounds to shoot out on the required trajectory. These mortars were impossible to detect from the air and impervious to anything short of a direct hit down the hole from a heavy bomb or large-calibre shell. Since 881S was a fixed target, such underground positions were entirely feasible, because, at that range, a minute change in the horizontal or vertical alignment of the tube was enough to ensure that any point on the hill could be fired on. Even the thud of a mortar firing was muffled by the depth of the emplacement, so that a report, readily audible had the tube been out in the open, could only be heard on the hill by a practised ear and only when all else was quiet – no nearby aircraft, no impacting artillery, no strong wind – a rarity on the Khe Sanh plateau.

At first, our resupply was provided by single helicopter from Khe Sanh. The pilot would ask that the troops be up in the trenches, firing to suppress the numerous anti-aircraft guns whose rounds swept across the hilltop landing zones

Below: A US Skyraider pulls up after bombing a North Vietnamese artillery piece near the Khe Sanh perimeter.
Far right: A Marine A-4 Skyhawk, with full bomb-load, prepares to take off on a mission. Navy, Marine and Air Force aircraft all contributed to the defence of Khe Sanh. Air power inflicted heavy casualties on the North Vietnamese and also devastated their morale.

from north and south. The result, however, was catastrophic, for, as soon as the pilot committed the helicopter to a zone, the North Vietnamese forward observer relayed the zone location to his mortarmen, who knew from long practice the exact range to each zone, and were able to fire precisely aimed rounds in seconds, unheard on the hill because of the noise of the helicopter. The time of flight for the rounds was about 25 seconds, and to unload supplies and load up the wounded within that time was impossible. On the 22nd, two rounds bracketed the zone just as the last wounded man was being loaded aboard a medevac helicopter, and 22 men were killed or grievously wounded, including the helicopter crew. The aircraft, with its cargo of wounded Marines, was completely destroyed.

By early February, the combined effects of the mortars and the incessant anti-aircraft fire had cost the Marines of Companies India and Mike 150 casualties and six helicopters. Including the toll of men shot by snipers, the casualty rate was over 50 per cent, with no end in sight. At that rate, the position would soon have become untenable, for replacements were sometimes hit before they even got off the incoming helicopters, and the troops were down to one quart canteen of water per day, an unacceptable level for the climate. When NVA anti-aircraft guns were destroyed, as they frequently were by air attacks or fire from our own guns, they were replaced as quickly as were the snipers.

The solution was unusual, probably impossible for any other military service in the world, and was instantly and consistently effective. A carefully rehearsed, perfectly timed and coordinated air–ground resupply operation, known as the 'Super Gaggle', was mounted on the first clear day in mid-February. On a pre-arranged signal, the mortar tubes on 881S opened up with white phosphorus shells, pre-registered against known anti-aircraft emplacements. Within seconds of the rounds' impacts, a flight of four Marine A-4 Skyhawk attack jets, each with several 5in anti-tank rockets mounted beneath its wings, dived from altitude and systematically attacked the emplacements, using the smoke from the phosphorus shells as a marker.

As soon as the first aircraft had unleashed their rockets and departed, a second flight of four A-4s, this time carrying napalm, bracketed the hill, close in, with sheets of fire to kill or discourage the North Vietnamese who in the past had frequently lain on their backs in shallow holes, just outside the defensive barbed wire, and fired automatic weapons into the bellies of the approaching helicopters. Close behind came two more A-4s, one on either side of the hill, dropping

Below: Marine medics remove the body of a helicopter crewman from the wreckage of his aircraft. The North Vietnamese destroyed 17 helicopters during the battle of Khe Sanh.
Far right, top: A C-46 lifts off from one of the hill posts. The landing zones at these positions were often subjected to heavy shelling while loading or unloading was in progress. Mortar rounds landing near men crowded round a helicopter would take a heavy toll of casualties.
Far right, below: A chaplain gives the last rites to a badly wounded victim of the hill fighting.

On 26 February 1968 a single US Air Force B-52 took off from U Tapao airbase for Khe Sanh. Its mission was to test out a close-in attack on North Vietnamese positions around the besieged combat base, using the 108 500lb bombs it carried. The test was a success. The next day four more close-in missions were flown, using Combat Skyspot, a computer system that guided the incoming bombers onto their targets. All the bombs fell within the designated target boxes and as the detonations of hundreds of bombs exploding simultaneously shook the earth at Khe Sanh, Marines emerged from their shelters to cheer the passing B-52s. During March B-52 close-in strikes became routine, and the records of the USAF 3rd Air Division indicate that during the siege some 2548 sorties were flown, with 59,249 tons of bombs dropped. To estimate the number killed by B-52 bombardment would be impossible. Captured documents indicate that at least 300 North Vietnamese deserted because of these attacks.

canisters of delayed-fuse bomblets which scattered the length of the flanking valleys and detonated at irregular intervals for several minutes thereafter.

There was then a momentary pause during which each mortarman fired several more rounds of white phosphorus in quick succession to blind whatever anti-aircraft guns the air attacks might not have destroyed. No fire from the hill, other than the mortars, was attempted. All other troops stayed under cover in individual man-sized holes dug into the uphill side of the trench bottom, with up to 10ft of dirt and rock over their heads.

The NVA mortarmen never again hit a zone with a helicopter in it

Through the haze of dust and smoke that constantly shrouded the plateau, there would then appear 10 Marine CH-46 medium helicopters, each bearing an externally slung load of 3000lb of supplies. As the helicopters neared 881S, four more A-4s would scream by, two on either flank, laying a screen of thick white smoke between 881S and the ridges to the north and south on which the NVA anti-aircraft guns were positioned. The effect was to create a narrow valley of visibility over the hill, into which the 10 helicopters descended, in echelons of five, to release their loads and climb away quickly into the smoke on the upwind side. Usually, in the rear echelon of helicopters that followed a few seconds behind the first, one aircraft would land in a predetermined zone with replacement men, prepared to pick up the waiting casualties. The position of the aircraft in the echelon and the zone it would use were varied constantly, and the blinded North Vietnamese mortarmen were never again successful in hitting a zone with a helicopter and men in it.

The entire Super Gaggle operation took less than five minutes, and from the laying of the shielding smoke to the departure of the last helicopter was never more than 30 seconds. Anti-aircraft fire still swept the hill, but in substantially less volume, unaimed, and therefore ineffective. Mortar rounds still rained down, often for up to an hour after the aircraft had departed, but they were at most a nuisance, for the Marines in their burrows kept their heads down. Some 30,000lb of supplies were scattered across the hill, replacement troops were in, and the wounded were out, usually without a casualty. The entire operation was controlled from a two-seat TA-4 jet, flown by the A-4 squadron commander with the helicopter squadron commander in the back seat and radio contact with myself on the hill. These were all Marines who had trained, marched and partied together for years, and so could make such a complex, split-second operation work.

After dark, when the North Vietnamese could no longer observe us, we gathered the supplies, which were often riddled by shrapnel from the post-Gaggle mortaring, distributed them, and set the watch to ward off any attack. The

Above: Lance-Corporal Molikau Niuatoa (left) guided US aircraft onto a North Vietnamese artillery position using 20-power naval binoculars.
Left: An A-4 Skyhawk drops its bombload.

KHE SANH – FACTS AND FIGURES

The US combat base at Khe Sanh was situated in the northernmost province of South Vietnam, some 15 miles south of the Demilitarized Zone and 6 miles east of the border with Laos. Khe Sanh was established as one of a series of fire bases, known as the McNamara Line, that stretched from the coast to the Laotian border. Its purpose was to cut troop and supply infiltration into South Vietnam from the North and to block North Vietnamese incursions from Laos. In early January 1968, US intelligence sources pointed to signs of a mounting North Vietnamese offensive in the northern provinces.

On the base the Marine commanding officer, Colonel David E. Lownds, had at his disposal the 1st, 2nd and 3rd Battalions, 26th Marine Regiment, and an artillery unit, the 1st Battalion, 13th Marines. As the siege developed, the battalions of the 26th and 13th Regiments were reinforced by the 1st Battalion, 9th Marines and the 37th Rangers (a South Vietnamese battalion).

It soon became clear that the NVA intended to hit Khe Sanh in strength. The battle for Khe Sanh opened on 22 January 1968 with a massive rocket, artillery and mortar bombardment that blew up 1340 tons of munitions in the main ammo dump. Throughout February the enemy continued to pour heavy fire into the base and onto the Marine positions on Hill 881S. The Leathernecks replied with bombs, cannon and napalm, culminating in March with massive close-in B-52 strikes. By the beginning of April, NVA attacks on the base began to fade as the US relief operation – Pegasus – came into effect. Khe Sanh was relieved on 8 April.

Estimates place the North Vietnamese strength during the siege at between 15,000 and 20,000 men. From 19 January to 31 March the Marines lost 199 men killed and 830 wounded; NVA losses were put as high as 10,000 – 15,000.

night watch was 50 per cent until midnight and all hands thereafter until dawn. The enemy could not set up for an attack until dusk without risk of detection, and movement to assault positions up the slopes of the hill would have taken until midnight. The Marines knew – they'd climbed it often enough themselves.

Hill 881S was never assaulted. There were occasional probes to the outer defensive wire, but these only served to prove that a Marine could throw a hand-grenade downhill far better than a North Vietnamese soldier could throw one uphill – and ours didn't come rolling back down on us. Both to conserve water and to avoid casualties, the Marines worked at night, with only small observation posts and the supporting-arms controllers about in daylight. Casualties, after the Gaggles began, were steady but light, for few Marines were above ground.

As their rate of fire decreased, so ours accelerated. The weather was improving, and attack aircraft could fly almost daily. Rocket sites were regularly attacked, and in an awesome display of patience and visual acuity, a young American Samoan, Lance-Corporal Molikau Niuatoa, using 20-power naval binoculars, spotted the flash of an artillery piece at a range of over 16,000yd to the west. He'd been watching for weeks, orientating on the boom of the guns as they fired over 881S onto the base. Corporal Robert Arrotta, India's forward air contoller, quickly sent an airborne observer to the area, but neither he nor Niuatoa could see the aircraft at that distance to guide it to the target.

Above, far left: Colonel David E. Lownds (left) commander of the Khe Sanh combat base, meets officers of the relief column that reached the base on 6 April 1968. Above: At the end of the long battle, Marines take time out to have a cup of coffee, served from old tin cans.

Above: A Marine radio operator perches on a sandbagged bunker at Khe Sanh.

With NVA artillery as the prize, the observer soon had several flights of bombers orbiting over him, waiting to receive his target data. He fired a white smoke marking rocket, but it could not be seen from Niuatoa's position on the hill through the haze. Finally, his bombers running low on fuel, the observer proposed that he unload a planeload of 500lb bombs on a prominent ridge. He did, and we saw their impact. Niuatoa's first correction, given in his typical laconic voice, would qualify as bold in any armed force: 'Left 1000 yards, add two ridgelines.' Patiently, using bomb strikes as marking rounds, he closed the bracket, and suddenly, the excited voice of the observer came over the radio: 'We found the bastards! We've got 'em!' By day's end he was able to report the destruction of five 130mm Soviet-made field guns, whose accuracy and 29,000yd range had been so damaging.

In March, as the siege of Khe Sanh wound down, Captain Harry Jenkins (commanding Mike Company) and I acted as the conductors of an orchestra. With radios as our 'batons' we orchestrated the unlimited and instantly available artillery and aircraft ordnance upon any movement, or sound, or smell, or hunch. The noise was constant. What had been a green rolling plateau three months earlier now looked more like the surface of the moon, with long series of overlapping craters and blasted stumps.

The siege did not end abruptly. Rather, the North Vietnamese simply melted away, with an occasional small pocket of diehards left behind for the relieving forces to mop up. A full-scale attack on the Khe Sanh base was never mounted. An incident on 881S, around 1 April, as the relieving forces arrived, perhaps shows why. Two naked North Vietnamese soldiers ran up to our wire in broad daylight, waving propaganda leaflets to indicate surrender. One was shot in the back by his comrades, and the other went to ground outside the wire until a Marine, under our covering fire, crawled across and led him to the safety of the trench. He was an impressive man, almost six foot tall, healthy looking, and of imposing physique. We began to question him, but were interrupted by his amazing transformation as a Marine jet passed overhead. He literally lost complete control of himself – his muscles, his eyes, even his bowels – and fell in a quivering heap to the bottom of the trench. Even a loud handclap behind him would produce that same petrified reaction. The man had been psychologically destroyed by the awesome pounding he and his comrades had been subjected to during the preceding 77 days. If he was anywhere near typical of the soldiers surrounding us, and in the rare moments when he was lucid he said that he was, it was no wonder they could not mount an assault.

India returned to the coast with only 19 of the 200 original Marines who had taken up the defence of 881S. Mike had fared little better. Sent to a supposedly secure cantonment as Quang Tri the night we flew east, we lost six more of those 19 from India Company when a rocket struck the ridgepole of a tent to which they had been assigned. The defence of Khe Sanh had been successful – but costly.

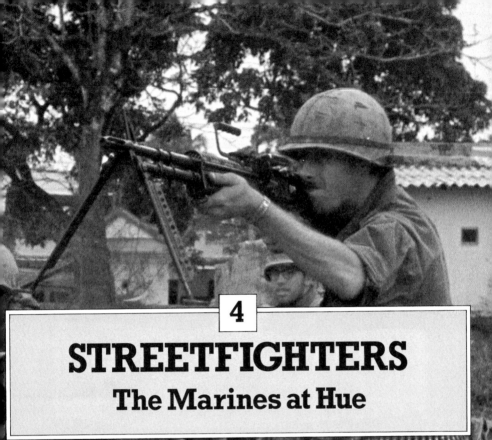

4
STREETFIGHTERS
The Marines at Hue

DURING THE afternoon of 31 January 1968, Lieutenant-Colonel Marcus Gravel, commander of the 1st Battalion, 1st Marine Regiment, led his men across the fire-swept Nguyen Hoang bridge, into the Old City of Hue. Supported by tanks (which were unable to follow because of their vulnerability in close-quarters urban fighting), Gravel found that he was facing far more enemy firepower than he could cope with. Commandeering some trucks, he pulled back with his wounded. The involvement of the US Marines in the fighting for Hue had begun.

Hue was the most important city in the northern provinces of South Vietnam. It was often called the 'Imperial City'

NVA assault

Jan NVA infiltrators join Viet Cong units in Hue in preparation for Tet Offensive.
31 Jan 0340 Communist forces launch a rocket and mortar attack. They advance on the ARVN HQ in the north of the Old City. The elite ARVN 'Black Panther' company is deployed but it is driven back.

Perfume r

Clearing the Old City

12 Feb 1st Battalion, 5th Marin deployed in the Old City by land craft and helicopter to break th stalemate there. Other US force squeeze the NVA from the east Bitter house-to-house fighting continues for two more weeks.
21 Feb Imperial Palace in Sout Vietnamese hands.
22-24 Feb Final attacks go in. L and South Vietnamese forces g control of Hue.

PLANNING THE OFFENSIVE

In July 1967, a high-level conference was convened in Hanoi under the auspices of Ho Chi Minh, the President of North Vietnam, and his military commander, General Vo Nguyen Giap. Its brief was to consider how to break the military stalemate in the Vietnam War.

After protracted discussion, it was decided that a massive offensive should be launched against South Vietnam in early 1968 using the combined might of the regular North Vietnamese Army (NVA) and the Viet Cong, the military arm of the National Liberation Front (NLF). The attack was designed with three aims in mind: to encourage a popular anti-government rising in the South, to bring about the collapse of the South Vietnamese government and seriously to undermine the military and political standing of the US in Vietnam. A less obvious element in North Vietnamese thinking was to assert control over the Viet Cong by committing them to a battle that would leave them weakened.

The assault was planned to be as widespread as possible, with the NVA attacking the northern provinces and the Viet Cong striking at every major town and village in South Vietnam. The decision to attack during the Tet (Lunar New Year) celebrations at the end of January 1968 was significant. Giap believed that, with many soldiers on leave, the South Vietnamese would be caught off balance and that bad weather might make it impossible for the US to fly close-support missions.

In the weeks prior to the New Year, the NVA and Viet Cong continued to mount their regular operations to disguise the concentration of their forces but, by the end of January, all was ready and on the 31st the Tet Offensive began. Over 84,000 NVA and Viet Cong troops attacked 36 provincial capitals, 64 district capitals and 50 villages in South Vietnam. The focal point of the attack in the northern coastal provinces was the old imperial city of Hue.

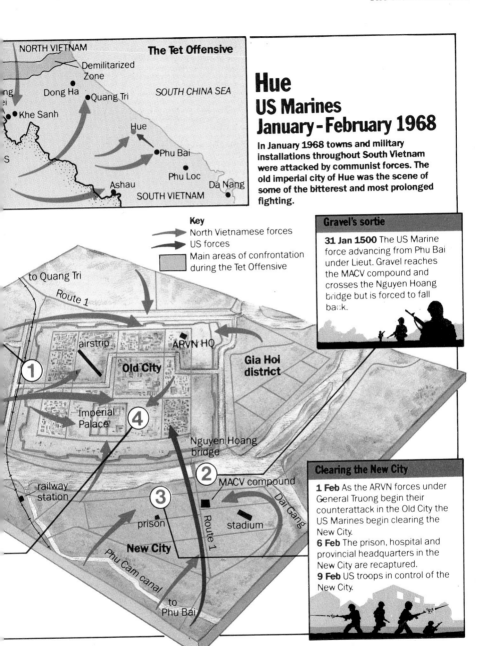

The Tet Offensive

NORTH VIETNAM

Demilitarized Zone

Dong Ha • Quang Tri

SOUTH CHINA SEA

• Khe Sanh

Hue

• Phu Bai

Phu Loc •

Ashau

Da Nang •

SOUTH VIETNAM

Hue
US Marines
January - February 1968

In January 1968 towns and military installations throughout South Vietnam were attacked by communist forces. The old imperial city of Hue was the scene of some of the bitterest and most prolonged fighting.

Gravel's sortie

31 Jan 1500 The US Marine force advancing from Phu Bai under Lieut. Gravel reaches the MACV compound and crosses the Nguyen Hoang bridge but is forced to fall back.

Key

North Vietnamese forces

US forces

Main areas of confrontation during the Tet Offensive

to Quang Tri

Route 1

airstrip

ARVN HQ

Old City

Gia Hoi district

①

Imperial Palace

④

railway station

Nguyen Hoang bridge

② MACV compound

Dai Gang

③

prison

Route 1

stadium

New City

Phu Cam canal

to Phu Bai

Clearing the New City

1 Feb As the ARVN forces under General Truong begin their counterattack in the Old City the US Marines begin clearing the New City.
6 Feb The prison, hospital and provincial headquarters in the New City are recaptured.
9 Feb US troops in control of the New City.

Page 67: An M60 machine-gunner in an infantry squad gives covering fire.

COMMUNIST FORCES

The Army of the Republic of Vietnam (ARVN) and its US allies faced two distinct military opponents during the 1968 Tet Offensive: the well-trained regulars of the North Vietnamese Army (NVA) – controlled from Hanoi – and the Viet Cong (VC), an experienced guerrilla army based in the South Vietnamese countryside. Although both were committed to the overthrow of the Republic of South Vietnam, led by President Nguyen Van Thieu, the leadership of the two forces differed over the strategy of the war after the arrival of US combat troops. Hanoi was more concerned with finding a war-winning tactic to offset American firepower, and the VC were left to provide the backbone of the Tet Offensive. They were reinforced for the operation by men from VC regional units that normally confined their operations to their home province.

Equipment of the VC and the NVA was identical, predominantly of Soviet and Chinese origin. The AK-47, manufactured in China, the Soviet Union or other Warsaw Pact nations, was the most common smallarm of a heterogeneous collection. Soviet-designed SKS carbines and the North Vietnamese K50 sub-machine gun were also frequently used.

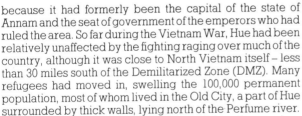

Left: Armed with M16s, a group of Marines awaits the order to join battle.
Below left: An officer of the NVA shouts encouragement to his men.
Below: A Marine officer, armed with his Colt .45, ducks behind cover to avoid sniper fire.

because it had formerly been the capital of the state of Annam and the seat of government of the emperors who had ruled the area. So far during the Vietnam War, Hue had been relatively unaffected by the fighting raging over much of the country, although it was close to North Vietnam itself – less than 30 miles south of the Demilitarized Zone (DMZ). Many refugees had moved in, swelling the 100,000 permanent population, most of whom lived in the Old City, a part of Hue surrounded by thick walls, lying north of the Perfume river.

The decision to attack Hue had been taken the previous summer. The North Vietnamese and their southern allies, the Viet Cong, had made up their minds to undertake a large-scale offensive against the major towns in the South, in an attempt to destroy the morale of the Army of the Republic of Vietnam (ARVN) and provoke an uprising against the government.

The Tet Offensive, as the series of attacks in late January 1968 became known, was not entirely unexpected, but the scale and intensity of the attacks were. Not only that, but the attention of all US troops in Vietnam, and especially the Marines, was concentrated on Khe Sanh, the beleaguered combat base that had been under siege since 21 January.

Above: US Marines regroup after clearing VC troops out of a building near the Citadel at Hue.

Indeed, on 25 January, the US forces in the northern provinces had been planning the relief of Khe Sanh, not preparing to defend against assaults on key urban areas.

The crump of mortars and the roar of rockets heralded the assault

In the early morning of 31 January, the crump of mortars and the roar of rockets heralded the opening of an assault by North Vietnamese Army (NVA) forces against Hue. The few ARVN forces that were stationed in the city belonged to Brigadier-General Ngo Quang Truong's 1st Division and were of good quality. They had realised that there was the possibility of an attack, and so were at full alert; and the 'Black Panther' Company managed to slow considerably the advance of two NVA infantry battalions and their sapper support as they drove into the Old City from the southwest. With solid support from local Viet Cong units, however, the NVA troops soon controlled almost all the Old City. Only the far northern corner, the site of Truong's divisional headquarters, still held out by the time dawn broke.

Meanwhile, in the part of Hue south of the Perfume river known as the 'New City', the attacking troops were also successful. Viet Cong squads took over key government

Right: Marines of the 2nd Battalion, 5th Marines pause for a smoke after clearing and securing the building in the background.

buildings, and although the Americans in the headquarters compound of MACV (Military Assistance Command Vietnam, the official title of the US command in Vietnam) held out, there were only a few other isolated pockets of resistance. The attack on the Imperial City had been a great success. Well-armed, well-trained, and knowing exactly what they had to do, the communist forces had taken most of their objectives, and NVA battalions now began to fan out, to take up blocking positions to the north and south of the city, while the Viet Cong flag, gold stars on red and blue, was soon flying defiantly over the old Imperial Palace.

The nearest US Marine units were at the Phu Bai combat base, some 8 miles to the south. There, Task Force X-Ray, under Brigadier-General Foster Lahue (a veteran of the Marines of World War II and a battalion commander in Korea) was composed of the headquarters detachments of the 1st and 5th Marine Regiments, and three understrength battalions (at full strength, Task Force X-Ray should have included two whole regiments – six battalions). Lahue's 4000 men were tasked with the defence of Phu Bai itself, the screening of the western approaches to Hue, and the maintenance of traffic along Route 1, from Hai Van Pass to Hue. Route 1 was the key north–south land communications

Streetfighters

route from Da Nang to Hue; it had already come under rocket and mortar attack during the night of the 31st.

Reports were flowing in of a major offensive throughout South Vietnam, including an assault on the US embassy in Saigon, and that morning Lahue had to take some critical decisions. He sent Company A, 1st Battalion, 1st Marines, towards Hue to investigate the situation on Route 1 and to link up with the MACV compound in the New City. Company A quickly ran into trouble, however. NVA troops were waiting in ambush, and the Marines had barely covered half the distance to Hue when they became pinned down.

By mid-morning on the 31st, Lahue had realised that Company A needed support, and so Lieutenant-Colonel Marcus Gravel, with the command group of 1st Battalion, 1st Marines, and Company G, 2nd Battalion, 5th Marines, was sent out. A tank platoon and some engineers provided

support. Gravel was able to use this small force to push a way through the NVA screen and, although under fire from Viet Cong and NVA elements within Hue itself, he crossed the bridge over the Phu Cam canal and entered the MACV compound just before 1500 hours.

Having got this far, Gravel was ordered to try to make contact with the ARVN units under Brigadier-General Truong who were holding out in the northern corner of the Old City. His men moved over the Nguyen Hoang bridge, but without heavy support they could make little headway in the Old City, and pulled back.

That night the chaotic situation all over Vietnam became clearer; and within Hue itself the possibility of further large-scale communist assaults began to recede. The next day, therefore, Gravel again tried to force a way through to Truong's headquarters, only to meet renewed resistance

Above: Lieutenant-Colonel Marcus Gravel, CO of the first Marines into Hue.

Right: A Marine crouches in a sewer while giving covering fire with an M60 machine gun. Other members of his squad drag a wounded comrade into cover for medical attention. Nearly 1000 Marines were killed or wounded in the month-long fighting at Hue.

LEAVING HUE

At the height of the fighting for Hue, landing craft became a major form of transport in and out. These journeys were frequently dangerous, as the communist forces controlled key areas on the banks of the Perfume river, and enemy mortar spotters would quickly call up fire when the landing craft docked. One journalist wrote:
'The mortar men were lousy shots. Two shells fell in the river, kicking up small geysers of water. A third one his a packing crate, well away from the craft....
'When the last crate was hauled from the craft, the passengers rushed aboard. The women, children and the stretcher cases were taken below the main deck. The others, including wounded Marines who could still walk, squatted on the deck in the rain. It was a strange cargo. There were two priests, who had been held captive by the Viet Cong; the bodies of six Marines in green plastic bags; and a group of teachers who had been trapped for nine days in Hue....
'"If you've got weapons, you ought to get them ready," one crewman told the passengers. "It will be a miracle if we don't have to use them." There was no miracle. Ten minutes out of Hue, Viet Cong troops ran along the riverbank firing rifles and rockets at the lumbering landing craft. The wounded Marines rushed to the ship's railing, firing steadily....
'A half-an-hour later, when the shooting had subsided, one of the passengers reached under his coat, pulled out a bottle of Ambassador Scotch and passed it around to the Marines. They emptied it in four minutes...'

Right: This Marine wears olive-drab drill fatigues and, for protection against blast weapons, he has an M1955 armoured vest. His boots are the tropical pattern, made of nylon and black leather. The camouflage cover of his M1 steel helmet bears graffiti expressing a common 'grunt' sentiment; a bottle of insect repellent is stuck in the helmet band. He is armed with the 5.56mm M16 assault rifle and spare magazines are carried in the cotton bandolier slung over his left shoulder.

Below: One member of an M60 machine-gun team fires the weapon while the other feeds a belt of ammo. The gunner has a toothbrush and bottle of oil in his helmet band for maintenance of his weapon in the field.

from the NVA troops digging in within the walls of the Old City.

Meanwhile, more Marine forces were arriving: by 4 February, Colonel Stanley Hughes, the regimental commander of the 1st Marines, had come in to take charge of the two battalions of Marines who had been ordered to clear Hue south of the Perfume river. The battalions consisted of those units from the 1st Marines that had already gone into action with Gravel, and three rifle companies, F, G and H, from the 5th Marines, now under their own battalion commander, Lieutenant-Colonel Ernest Cheatham.

Hughes was an officer with considerable World War II experience, having won both a Navy Cross and a Silver Star for his service in that conflict; and the battle that was to follow was in many ways more like some of the more gruelling episodes of the war against the Japanese on the Pacific Islands than anything that had been experienced in Vietnam so far. For the communist forces holed up in the city were not going to slip away to fight another day. They had been ordered to hold on until the bitter end, and they would have to be winkled out, house by house, bunker by bunker.

Most of the Marines at Hue were short-term enlistees, and, although they had been trained to operate in a number of environments, they expected to fight the Viet Cong in the countryside where they could call upon enormous resources of firepower and had the great advantage of superior mobility. Now, however, they faced a different kind of warfare: close-quarters, almost hand-to-hand combat with movement confined to swift dashes across fire-swept streets, dodging from one scrap of cover to another, with enemy snipers liable to pick off anyone careless enough to show himself, and with heavy support sometimes an irrelevance. Heaps of rubble were just as useful as complete buildings in providing shelter for the defenders, and so blanket shelling was of limited value. Just as in the great close-quarters battles of World War II – Stalingrad, Cassino or Iwo Jima – the attacking infantry had to fight their way in and pull out the defenders one by one.

The attacking infantry had to put up an enormous weight of covering fire to support even short advances, and the dull pink buildings characteristic of Hue were soon pockmarked by the deluge of fire that the Marines put up to keep the heads of the NVA down while the American troops moved forward. The M16 assault rifle, which many Marines had regarded somewhat dubiously when it first came into service, proved invaluable in Hue, as its fully automatic mode gave a powerful burst that could keep defenders under pressure.

The communists had turned all the government buildings into strongpoints

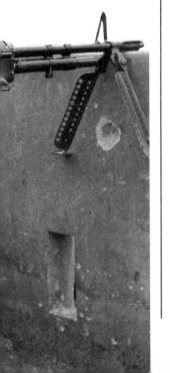

For their part, the communist forces had turned all the government buildings they had occupied in the New City into strongpoints. Snipers took to the upper stories, while machine-gun nests were set up lower down. Mortars were carefully sited to cover approach routes, and dug in to avoid detection, while the infantrymen settled into small 'spider holes', nursing extra magazines for their AK-47s.

There was no 'front line' as such when the fighting began in Hue; Viet Cong sabotage squads and courageous solo snipers were an ever-present threat. Indeed, soon after the Marine clearing of the New City began, saboteurs blew up the bridge over the Phu Cam canal, which meant that supplies had to be brought in by helicopter or up the river. Both of these methods were fraught with peril. Slow-moving helicopters were vulnerable to ground fire if they strayed over a communist-held area, while shipping coming up the Perfume river had to run the gauntlet of NVA gun positions sited along the banks.

Five Landing Craft, Utility (LCUs), brought the bulk of equipment and ammunition in until the Phu Cam canal was rebridged on 12 February, and they suffered heavily. Two loaded with petrol, oil and lubricants caught fire and sank under enemy attack from the banks of the Perfume river and an LCU loaded with ammunition blew up when communist

The Marines at Hue fought in one of the toughest infantry battles of the Vietnam War and suffered very high casualties in the confused street fighting. In Vietnam the proportion of fatal wounds from smallarms fire averaged around 51 per cent, a much higher figure than in World War II or the Korean War where artillery and aerial bombardment accounted for the majority of fatal casualties. This was due to the high-velocity, lightweight bullets of modern assault rifles which left large entry and exit wounds. America has always honoured those wounded in the line of duty and the Purple Heart (shown above) is awarded to those who have received injuries in action.

troops managed to get it in their sights. South of the river, helicopters were able to alight at relatively protected Landing Zones (LZs), but in the Old City there was always a problem. The only effective LZ was at the hospital, and craft landing there were always liable to be fired on. Only one Marine helicopter was actually lost in a total of 823 sorties, but many received multiple hits.

The problem of moving supplies and reinforcements into Hue was mirrored by the difficulties of shifting wounded men to safety. The prospect of being lifted out by a helicopter vulnerable to enemy smallarms fire, or travelling on an LCU after the episode of the blown-up ammunition carrier was far from welcome.

The Marines had some support from M48 tanks (which did remarkably well in the street fighting – only one Marine tank was lost) and the 'Ontos', a thinly armoured, tracked vehicle mounting six recoilless rifles, proved an invaluable asset, deploying a great weight of firepower against defensive positions at close range. The Ontos could enter areas that the

Left: A casualty receives medical attention at a field dressing station. Below: Marine medics carry a casualty to a landing zone for helicopter evacuation. Several Marine helicopters were heavily damaged in evacuating the wounded, but only one was shot down.

Above: The desperate street fighting in Hue wore at the nerves of the Marines engaged in combat. This man shows the strain on his face as he rests under cover during a lull in the battle.

larger, heavier tanks could not; it would dart out, send in a shattering salvo, and then pull back under cover.

One Marine unit, Major Robert Thompson's 1st Battalion, 5th Marines, was deployed into the Old City to support Truong's ARVN force operating there; and this battalion had an even more difficult task than those south of the river. For the greater density of buildings and the greater determination of the defenders made this part of the fighting a grim struggle indeed.

The period of the battle for Hue coincided with the northeast monsoon. The skies were generally overcast and the atmosphere heavy, severely hindering any close air support. For the Marines, the days spent fighting in Hue under these grey, leaden skies assumed a kind of routine. They would force their way forward during the day, struggling to prise the communist forces out of their concealed defences, bringing up what support weapons they could to help them in their grim task, and then hope to catch a hot meal at night. But during the night, the NVA and the Viet Cong would launch local counter-attacks, and individual communist troops who had remained hidden would emerge to set lethal booby traps.

Crouching behind walls, setting up as much covering fire as they could, the Marines inched forward, haggard with fatigue. In the New City, the US forces began to assert control within a week: the building housing the administrative headquarters of the province was retaken by 6 February, as were the prison and the hospital. By 9 February, all organised resistance south of the Perfume river had been crushed. For Thompson's 1st Battalion, 5th Marines, on the northern bank helping Truong's forces in the Old City, things were more difficult. But by 21 February the flag of South Vietnam was flying again over the Imperial Palace, and on 22 February the final attacks went in, with Marine aircraft using the opportunity of a break in the cloud cover to deliver a devastating weight of ordnance on the southern corner of the Old City in support of Thompson's troops, dropping 250lb 'Snakeye' bombs and 500lb napalm canisters.

In spite of the fact that close support was always difficult, the Marines had used their superior firepower wherever possible. Marine artillery fired 18,091 rounds during the battle: high explosive, smoke, white phosphorus, illumination and CS gas. The accuracy of the 8in howitzer made it the most effective artillery piece. From the Seventh Fleet, three cruisers and five destroyers expended 5191 rounds, and, although the weather limited their effectiveness, Marine aircraft flew 113 sorties.

The unexpected determination of Viet Cong and NVA forces to fight to the last inch, and the fact that street fighting was an unusual problem in the Vietnam War, made the fighting in Hue the bitterest that any of the rank and file Marines had ever experienced; and they suffered 142 dead in the struggle to reclaim the city. But they had proved yet again the fighting qualities of their Corps, in adverse conditions and against a determined enemy.

5

INTERNATIONAL POLICEMEN
The Marines Today

After the end of the Vietnam War, the Corps once again returned to what it regarded as its primary role, that of an amphibious assault force. It took delivery of M60 tanks and British-designed AV-8 jump-jets to provide heavy support for its assault force. Orders were also placed for many high-technology weapons (including F-14 fighters, although these were eventually cancelled), and the Corps' anti-tank capability was improved with the introduction into service of the TOW (tube-launched, optically-sighted, wire-guided) and Dragon missiles. In an attempt to select recruits better suited to the demands of modern, high-technology warfare, good performance on the armed services' aptitude test replaced the previous demand for a high-school diploma. In the late 1970s, however, the diploma qualification was reinstated. In 1986 the Marine Corps totalled 198,241 personnel (including 9,200 women). There were three divisions and three Marine Air Wings. The Corps could deploy 760 M60A1 tanks, 984 LVTP-7/-7A1 amphibious personnel carriers, and over 300 artillery pieces of various calibres. The Air Wings had some 600 combat aircraft, including 141 F-4 Phantoms, 52 AV-8A/Cs, 197 A-4 Skyhawks, 69 A-6 Intruders, and 92 F/A-18 Hornets. Over 100 helicopters were also available.

THE LAST Marine ground troops left South Vietnam on 25 June 1971, but Marine air units continued operations against North Vietnamese and Viet Cong forces until the ceasefire in January 1973. The Marines' experience of Vietnam was not yet at an end, however. The collapse of South Vietnam and Cambodia during the 1975 offensives forced the evacuation of US embassy personnel from their respective capitals, Saigon and Phnom Penh. The Marines involved in the evacuations belonged to the Marine Security Guard Batta-

lion, which provides guards for US embassies. They were reinforced from units stationed with the Seventh Fleet.

In Phnom Penh, on 12 April 1975, the Marines secured a football field near the embassy. This was used as a landing zone for the helicopters brought in from USS *Okinawa* to evacuate embassy personnel and prominent Cambodians. This operation, Eagle Pull, took four hours to remove the entire embassy staff plus 159 Cambodians from the besieged city. As the Marines prepared to go, they came under mortar and rocket fire but there were no casualties. Phnom Penh fell to the Khmer Rouge on 14 April 1975.

Throughout April 1975 the United States had been conducting a slow evacuation of South Vietnamese orphans and persons associated with the Thieu regime. By the end of the month, however, North Vietnamese forces had gained possession of most of the country except for Saigon. The US ambassador, Graham Martin, still kept the evacuation on a small scale in the hope of avoiding widespread panic. But the North Vietnamese forced his hand on 28 April when they shelled Tan Son Nhut, Saigon's main airport. Two Marine Security Guards were killed. Ambassador Martin now requested President Gerald Ford to authorise the final evacuation of Saigon, and Operation Frequent Wind began.

The Marines of 2nd Battalion, 4th Marines (who had also been used during the Phnom Penh evacuations) were flown in to Tan Son Nhut. They secured a perimeter, and the evacuation proceeded despite steady fire from the North Vietnamese forces around the city. Marines of this unit were also flown to the embassy to assist the Security Guard Battalion in restraining the crowds of Vietnamese who had gathered around the compound in the hope of being lifted out of doomed Saigon. At the embassy, Marines were forced to use rifle butts on their erstwhile allies, driving them back from the walls. At 0800 on 30 April, the last 11 Marines were flown off the embassy roof aboard a CH-46 helicopter.

The President ordered the Marines to conduct an assault

The Corps was called upon to perform one more duty in the wake of the collapse of the United States' allies in southeast Asia. The cargo ship *Mayaguez*, owned by an American company, was seized by Khmer Rouge forces. The ship was boarded near the island of Poulo Wai, 40 miles off the coast of Cambodia, and then taken to the nearby island of Koh Tang. The 39 members of the *Mayaguez*' crew were taken onto the island, and the Khmer Rouge government in Phnom Penh accused the US government of using the vessel as a spyship, and of violating Cambodia's territorial waters.

President Ford denounced the act as piracy. He held a meeting with the National Security Council, and an amphibious brigade of the 3rd Marine Division, stationed on Okinawa, was put on alert. The President and his Security Council ordered the Marines to conduct an assault to recover the ship and rescue the crew.

Page 83: Marines in LVTP-7s come ashore at Beirut for the second time in six weeks, on 29 September 1982.
Far left and above: Marines in Phnom Penh during the evacuation of US embassy personnel on 12 April 1975. This operation, Eagle Pull, took only four hours to complete.

Above: The *Mayaguez* is towed away by USS *Holt*. The container ship was carrying commercial goods and some supplies for US service and embassy personnel in Thailand when it was seized by a Cambodian gunboat off Poulo Wai island.

C-141 transport planes took the 2nd Battalion, 9th Marines from Okinawa to U Tapao Air Force Base in Thailand. Two assault parties were organised. One, of 48 men commanded by Major Raymond Porter, was to board the *Mayaguez* from a destroyer, while another of 180 men under Captain James Davis was to land on Koh Tang by helicopter and bring out the crew.

As the helicopters approached the landing zone they came under smallarms fire

Early in the morning of 15 May 1975, 11 Air Force helicopters lifted off from U Tapao. They carried the Marine landing forces. While the main body continued on to Koh Tang, three HH-53s peeled off and flew to the destroyer USS *Harold E. Holt*, which was sailing in the direction of the island. The Marines clambered down rope ladders to the decks of the *Holt* as the helicopters hovered over the ship. The *Holt* then sailed up to the *Mayaguez* and, at 0830, the Marines went over the rails onto the cargo ship. A search of the vessel revealed that there was no one aboard, although the presence of warm food in the galley indicated that someone had

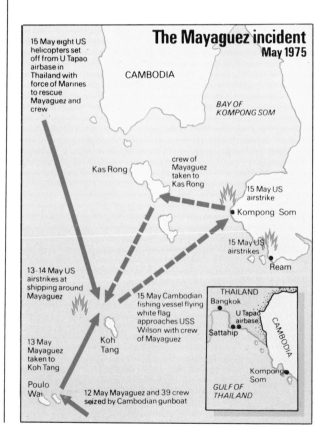

been there quite recently. The *Holt* then took the *Mayaguez* in tow and sailed off.

Covered by fighters from USS *Coral Sea*, the eight CH-53s and HH-53s carrying the main Marine assault force prepared to land the men on Koh Tang. The assault had two prongs, with a landing to be made on either side of the island's narrowest part. As the helicopters approached the landing zone at 0715 they came under smallarms fire from Khmer Rouge forces on the island. Of the first two helicopters approaching the eastern side of the island, one was hit and crashed into the sea, killing 13 men, while the other landed on the beach, its tail shot off. The Marines scrambled out of the wreck and took up defensive positions. Meanwhile, at the western landing zone the first two helicopters were also in trouble. One, carrying the company commander, was damaged and had to fly back to Thailand. The other managed to land its Marines, but crashed when it took off again, killing one of its crew.

The remaining four helicopters all flew to the western side, for the eastern landing zone was deemed too hot. Private, 1st Class Larry Yerg told *Newsweek* magazine: 'The landing zone was too hot for us to land, so they got us in as best they could. We wound up landing by the rocks. From the air, all I could see were straw-roofed huts and jungle. And the beach. Suddenly an AK-47 hit our helicopter and I realised that I was wounded in the left shoulder.'

Above: US Marines race into action on Koh Tang island. Intelligence sources had underestimated the number of Khmer Rouge soldiers on the island and the Marines met unexpectedly heavy resistance at the landing zone.

The Marines were under heavy fire from 200 Khmer Rouge fighters

---

The Marines on Koh Tang were now in three groups. One, of about 25 men, was at the eastern landing zone. Another 80 men were at the western landing zone. The remaining 29 men of the command group and mortar section were about 1300yd south of the main force. All were under heavy fire from an estimated 200 Khmer Rouge fighters. Lieutenant-Colonel Randall Austin, the battalion commander, told reporters afterwards that in some instances his men were throwing the enemy's grenades back at them. However, the heavy jungle of the island prevented the Marines from seeing the enemy clearly. The command group and the main body managed to link up, after a prolonged firefight, at about 0145. They now received reinforcements as a second wave was flown in, bringing a further 100 Marines.

Now these beleaguered men discovered that the crew of the *Mayaguez* was not on the island, but in fact aboard the USS *Henry B. Wilson*. The *Wilson* had found the 39 crew members aboard a Thai fishing boat at about 1100. Intelligence sources had failed to discover that the crew had been moved from Koh Tang, and that the Cambodian government had been preparing to release them anyway. The Marines' mission now changed from rescuing civilians to rescuing themselves.

Naval gunfire and air strikes were called on to force back the Khmer Rouge, but the Cambodians managed to bring such heavy fire to bear that helicopters were unable to land. The approach of darkness managed to reduce the effectiveness of enemy fire, and at 1710 the Marines on the eastern side were brought out by a single helicopter. With the help of a C-130 dropping a 15,000lb bomb, the men at the western landing zone were brought out in stages, the last 29 leaving at 2110. The casualty count for this operation totalled 41 US military personnel killed and 50 wounded.

Below left: A US Marine LVTP-7 parked in front of a Marine CH-Sea Knight helicopter on Grenada. The Marine role in Operation Urgent Fury, as an amphibious and helicopter-borne landing force, demonstrated that they had not forgotten the skills learned in World War II.

In October 1983 the Corps again went into action, in Operation Urgent Fury

The Marine Corps has always been used as a tool of US foreign policy in the Caribbean region. In this century it has been used to intervene on behalf of US interests in Panama, Mexico, Nicaragua and the Dominican Republic. In October 1983 the Corps once again went into action, in Operation Urgent Fury.

The island of Grenada had been thrown into turmoil by the removal from power and execution of its popular prime minister, Maurice Bishop, by a cabal of doctrinaire Marxist-Leninists led by Bernard Coard. The presence of US

citizens on the island – a group of medical students – gave the Reagan administration a pretext for intervention.

At 0530 on 25 October 1983, 500 men from the 22nd Marine Amphibious Unit aboard USS *Guam* made a vertical assault by helicopter on Pearls Airport on the eastern side of Grenada. It was part of a three-pronged assault on the island, as US Army Rangers and paratroops dropped onto Point Salines Airport while Navy SEALs (Sea, Air, Land troops) seized Government House, the residence of the Governor-General, Sir Paul Scoon. The Marines secured the airport in the face of light opposition by 0700.

The PRA had brought up three APCs to recapture the building

Grenadan resistance was stiffer on other parts of the island as Cuban workers (who had all received rudimentary training in their country's militia) teamed up with the Grenadan People's Revolutionary Army (PRA). The SEALs in Government House were in particular trouble, for the PRA had brought up three armoured personnel carriers to support their attempts to recapture the building. Some of the

Above: A Marine leads away Grenadan prisoners.
Below: Marines at ease after the end of Urgent Fury.

A posting to Beirut was an unenviable one at any time. At first, the Marines were faced with the boredom of a dull routine, but later, the constant sniping by smallarms and artillery exposed them to casualties, in a situation where the enemy was difficult to identify. The Marines patrolled an area of three square miles around Beirut international airport which was littered with unexploded shells from the previous spring's fighting, and the first Marine casualty was caused by the explosion of one of these during clearing operations. Once the Marines had set up camp, they began regular patrolling into the surrounding villages and suburbs. Some Lebanese locals greeted their presence, but others taunted them and displayed pictures of Ayatollah Khomeini. In the winter of 1982–83 the Marines lived in tents and found the Lebanese winter unexpectedly cold. Their main meals came from the US Navy ships offshore, and were supplemented by freeze-dried rations. The ships were also the Marines' main source of recreation: old films such as *Rocky II* were flown in nightly. Life for the Marines altered radically after the end of August 1983. The frequent sniping led to the construction of sandbagged emplacements. After the truck bombing in October 1983, perimeter security was strengthened, and most of the support personnel were withdrawn to the ships offshore.

Marines from Pearls Airport therefore re-embarked on the *Guam* and sailed around to St George's, the Grenadan capital, on the western side of the island.

Just before dawn on 26 October the Marines made an amphibious landing to the north of St George's. Red flares illuminated the beaches for the Marines coming ashore. Five M60 tanks and 13 LVTP-7 amphibious personnel carriers also landed, and, in the face of this, and carrier-borne air support, resistance waned rapidly.

The Marines set up a command post on St George's cricket ground as desultory fighting continued in the hills inland. They also secured Fort Rupert, the main military facility in the capital, capturing two Soviet-supplied anti-aircraft guns. By the evening of 27 October, most of the surviving Cubans and PRA men had been captured and the medical students had been evacuated by helicopter. Coard was later captured by a platoon of Marines and brought to trial on a conspiracy-to-murder charge. Operation Urgent Fury proved to be a great success, and a US-backed government came to power in Grenada in the elections of December 1984.

Public order in Beirut threatened to deteriorate into anarchy

The third major deployment of the Corps in the post-Vietnam era was as part of the Multi-National Force (MNF) in Lebanon. The MNF was originally formed to oversee the evacuation of Palestinian fighters from Beirut in the wake of Israel's 1982 invasion of Lebanon. Some 800 Marines drawn from the Sixth Fleet's attached Marine Amphibious Unit first landed in Beirut on 21 August 1982. This operation proceeded smoothly and the Marines were all withdrawn by 10 September. However, after the massacre of Palestinian refugees at the Sabra and Chatila camps in Beirut by Lebanese Christian Phalangists and members of the Israeli-supported Lebanese Force of the South, public order in Beirut threatened to deteriorate into anarchy. The Lebanese president, Amin Gemayel, invited the MNF to return and help in the restoration of Lebanese sovereignty in Beirut.

The Marines were scheduled to go in with the rest of the returning MNF on 21 September 1982, but the Israeli Army prevented this. The Israelis continued to occupy positions at Beirut's International Airport, where the Marines were to set up their base camp. President Reagan was forced to negotiate their withdrawal through his special envoy to the Israeli government, Morris Draper. The Marines were finally able to make their amphibious landing on 29 September 1982.

The boredom of the first winter in Beirut was relieved in January when Israeli Army forces began to harass the Marine positions. The most serious incident occurred on 2 February 1983. Three Israeli tanks attempted to drive through US positions on their way to another part of their lines. Captain Charles Johnson stood in their way and told them they could go no further. The Israeli commander, Lieutenant-Colonel 'Rafi' Lansberg, insisted on going through, and his tanks revved their engines to emphasise the point. Captain Johnson drew his pistol, loaded it, and waved it in the Israeli's face; once again Johnson told him he could not pass. The Israeli tanks withdrew.

Above, far left: US Marines come ashore in Beirut for the first time on 21 August 1982.
Below left: A Marine sniper in action in Beirut, January 1984.
Above and below: A Marine artillery observer sights for the battery of 155mm howitzers the Marines brought ashore with them in 1982.

Between March and August 1983, there was little action for the Marine force. This period was marred by one incident when a grenade was dropped from a first-story window onto a Marine patrol of 12 men; five Marines were slightly wounded. However, as the Israelis prepared to withdraw from Beirut in August, Shi'ite Moslems and their Druze allies began fighting the Gemayel government for control of west Beirut and the Chouf mountains. In the course of this fighting shells landed in the Marine base. Warning flares were fired and sometimes had the effect of stopping the shelling, but on 29 August two Marines were killed by mortar rounds. The Marine response was to use Huey Cobra gunships and 155mm howitzers to suppress the sources of the firing. However, after the Israeli withdrawal to the Awali river on 4 September, heavy fighting broke out.

President Reagan now authorised the US ships offshore to fire in support of the Marines, but, in the event, the first shelling from the ships was in support of the Lebanese Army. Any credibility that US military forces in Lebanon had as a neutral party was thus destroyed. The Marines had become legitimate targets for action in the eyes of the Druze and Shi'ites. Marine positions now came under regular fire from the Shi'ite slums around the airport, known to the Marines as either 'Hooterville' or 'Khomeiniville'. Mortars, rockets and smallarms fire killed three Marines and wounded several others in September and early October.

At 0620 on 23 October a Mercedes truck drove past two sentry posts and smashed into the four-story building serving as a Marine headquarters. Here the driver detonated the

Below: A Marine is pulled from the rubble of the Marine headquarters building by American and Lebanese rescue workers.
Far right: A Marine officer with a member of his command group in Beirut. The Reagan administration's Lebanese policies placed the Marines in the front line of a civil war. Despite being unsuited to the role they were called on to perform, their stoic suffering reminded Americans of the Corps' motto, *Semper fidelis* ('Always faithful').

2000lb of TNT in the truck. A massive explosion lifted the building off its foundations and, as it crashed back onto the ground, the structure collapsed upon the nearly 300 Marines using it as a barracks. Shocked Marines gathered around the ruins and began to pull their comrades from the rubble, desperately searching for survivors. Rescue efforts took place against a background of explosions as ammunition from a dump in the basement began to detonate. It took several days to clear the survivors and the bodies of the dead from the ruins. The final death toll was 241 Marines.

The Marine Corps has, from time to time, faced the threat of disbandment. Its abolition was first proposed in 1830, and the US Navy strongly supported moves to take the Marines off sea duty during the 1890s and 1900s. The most recent occasion when such ideas came under review was in the wake of the Vietnam War. In July 1975 the Senate Armed Services Committee instructed the Corps to re-evaluate its role: almost simultaneously the Brookings Institution, an important 'think-tank' based in Washington, D.C., began a similar study. The official Marine report emphasised the Marines' role as a quick reaction force, ready to contain a situation until the army could launch a major offensive. The Brookings study preferred a smaller Marine Corps operating in its traditional amphibious assault role. In 1977 the Carter administration asked the Pentagon to study the prospects of forming a rapid deployment force, which led to the formation of the Rapid Deployment Joint Task Force in 1979 with a strong Marine Corps presence. At present, the Marines' future is assured. The Reagan administration's military build-up has kept the Corps free of any budgetary cuts. The only cloud on the horizon is the formation by the US Army of a 'Light' Division, capable of rapid deployment to distant trouble spots. Could a future administration use this as a replacement for the Marine Corps?

There was another respite in the fighting during the month of November, giving the Marines time to collect themselves after the disaster of 23 October. In December firing on Marine positions resumed. The Marines had by now dug in deep, with sandbagged emplacements dotting what became known as 'Sand Bag City'. Tanks and light anti-tank weapons were now employed by the Marines when they came under fire. In the most serious incident, eight Marines were killed by a 120mm mortar bomb when they left their bunker to return enemy fire. The Marine commander regarded their conduct as 'understandable'.

It finally became obvious that the Marines' position was untenable

Skirmishes continued into January 1984, despite the support given by the 16in guns of USS *New Jersey*, which fired into the hills overlooking Beirut at the positions of the Druze artillery. However, as Lebanon slid once again into civil war it finally became obvious that the Marines' position was untenable. They withdrew between 22 and 26 February, and, as they went, the numerous mongrel dogs that had been adopted by the men of the base wandered forlornly among their departing masters. Sergeant Jeffrey Roberts observed to a *New York Times* reporter: 'They were the only real friends we had in Lebanon.' But, as usual, the Leathernecks had performed their thankless task with the grit and courage that typifies a truly great fighting elite.

CHRONOLOGY

1775 The Continental Congress authorizes the formation of two battalions of Marines.

1798 Congress authorizes the establishment of the United States' Marine Corps. A battalion of 880 Marines is formed.

1803 Marines operate against the Barbary pirates.

1805 Marines participate in the Eaton expedition against the town of Derna (now in Libya), assisting in its capture.

1812 Marines serve against Britain during the War of 1812.

1830 Congress defeats proposal of US President Andrew Jackson to incorporate the Marine Corps in the Army.

1847 Marines take part in the assault on Chapultepec Hill, later immortalized as the Halls of Montezuma, during the Mexican-American War.

1861 Outbreak of Civil War. Marines seize Hatteras Inlet, North Carolina, by amphibious assault.

1865 Civil War ends.

1898 Spanish-American War is fought. Marines seize Guantanamo Bay in Cuba by amphibious landing.

1916 The Corps is enlarged to 18,000 men.

1917 United States enters World War I. Marines arrive in France in June.

1918 The Marine Brigade participates in the battles of Belleau Wood, Soissons, St Mihiel and the Argonne. World War I ends.

1926 US Marines land in Nicaragua to protect American property endangered by civil disorder; they remain until 1933.

1941 Japanese attack Pearl Harbor; United States enters World War II.

1942 Marines defeat Japanese on Guadalcanal.

1943 Marines participate in campaigns in the Solomon Islands; battle of Tarawa.

1944 Marines involved in capture of Marshall, Mariana and Caroline Islands.

1945 Marines participate in capture of Iwo Jima and Okinawa. World War II ends.

1947 The size of the Marine Corps is fixed at 108,000 men.

1950 Korean War begins. Marines participate in the defence of the Pusan Perimeter, provide the spearhead for the landing at Inchon, and the fighting around the Chosin reservoir.

1953 The fighting in Korea ends.

1965 In March, two battalions of Marines land at Da Nang, South Vietnam; they conduct defensive operations around the US Air Force base there. In August, they begin to conduct offensive operations in northern South Vietnam.

1966 Marine forces in South Vietnam continue to be reinforced; they continue to perform search and destroy missions in the north of the country.

1968 North Vietnamese and Viet Cong launch Tet offensive. Marines fight in Khe Sanh and Hue battles.

1969 Marines begin troop withdrawals from South Vietnam.

1971 Last Marine ground troops leave South Vietnam.

1975 Marines participate in operation to rescue the crew of the *Mayaguez*.

1982 Marines begin peace-keeping operations in Beirut.

1983 Marines are involved in Urgent Fury, the operation to restore order on Grenada.

1984 Marines are withdrawn from Beirut.

FURTHER READING

Millett, Alan R. *Semper Fidelis: The History of the United States Marine Corps*, Macmillan, New York 1980

Moskin, J. Robert *The U.S. Marine Corps Story*, McGraw-Hill, New York 1982

Murphy, Jack *History of the US Marines*, Bison Books, London 1984

Russell, Lee E. *The US Marine Corps since 1945*, Osprey Publishing, London 1984

INDEX